FROM THE PUBLISHER ~~Antique Trader~~

POSTCARD COLLECTOR

GREETINGS FROM THE WAY WE WERE

BARBARA ANDREWS

Published by

Krause Publications, a division of F+W Media, Inc.
700 East State Street • Iola, WI 54990-0001
715-445-2214 • 888-457-2873
www.krausebooks.com

To order books or other products call toll-free 1-800-258-0929
or visit us online at www.krausebooks.com

ISBN-13: 978-1-4402-3498-9
ISBN-10: 1-4402-3498-1

Designed by Sharon Bartsch
Edited by Caitlin Spaulding

Printed in USA

CONTENTS

A NOTE ABOUT THE TEXT

Unless otherwise noted, the text in *Postcard Collector* is the work of Barbara Andrews. A renowned collector and beloved columnist for Antique Trader, Andrews has been relating post-card history, hobby tales, and collecting insights for over 35 years. Krause Publications is thrilled to be able to provide her readers with a complete volume of her work.

MORE GREAT TITLES
TO ENJOY,
from the publisher of *Antique Trader*:

Warman's Antiques and Collectibles 2013, 46th edition

Antique Trader Antiques & Collectibles Price Guide 2013

Antique Trader Bottles Identification & Price Guide, 7th Edition

Antique Trader Bottles Identification & Price Guide, 7th Edition

Warman's U.S. Stamps Field Guide, 2nd Edition

Picker's Bible, by Joe Willard

Fantastic Finds, by Eric Bradley

The Business of Antiques, by Wayne Jordan

To order books or other products call toll-free 1-800-258-0929
or visit us online at www.krausebooks.com

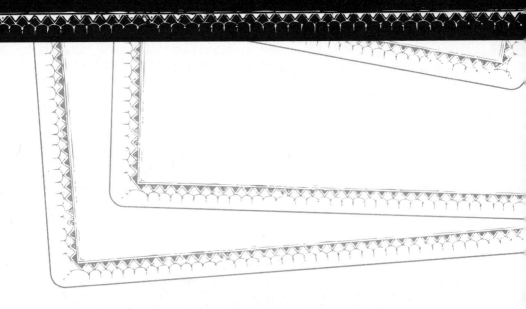

CHAPTER 1

TRENDS AND TALES

QUALITY POSTCARDS CAN BE FOUND IF YOU KNOW WHERE TO LOOK

Imagine walking across a field with a metal detector and finding $5 million worth of Roman coins. Dave Crisp of Wiltshire, England, did just that, amazing himself and the world with his find. Maybe there's a little treasure hunter in all of us, especially those who pursue antiques and collectibles.

Fortunately it's not necessary to tramp the countryside with a metal detector or dive on old shipwrecks to bring home a treasure trove. Anyone can play the game just by knowing the value of overlooked or undervalued objects.

Postcard collectors aren't likely to make a great find in old barns, sheds or junk yards, although my son once found some great old football cards at the city dump — before the trash master in charge chased him and his young friends away. His cards must have been a recent discard because they were in very good condition. Generally, though, the value of anything paper is destroyed by dampness, mold, pests or weathering. That doesn't mean a postcard collector can't strike it rich, even today when people are much more knowledgeable about the value of what they have.

The first step is to be sure the people in your circle of family and friends know what you collect.

My collection was greatly enriched by my father's acquaintances because he always said, "Send me a postcard," to anyone leaving on a trip. My greatest all-time buy came from a family friend who sold insurance. He visited in a lot of homes, and one of his clients showed him a suitcase full of early postcards. Yes, a suitcase! He only wanted the ones from Kalamazoo, so he showed the rest to me. I ended up buying them all for 5 cents each, but he didn't want to bother count-

No. 61. A Wylie Coach.

Photo by W. S. Berry, Gardiner, Mont.

ing them. He counted 100 and used the width to measure out the rest. Granted, that was quite a few years ago, but it was still a breathtaking treasure trove of early 1900s cards.

The point is, if my hobby hadn't been well known among my father's friends, I never would have had the opportunity to buy them. The same was true with my friends and family. My collection has been greatly enriched over the years by people who didn't care about old postcards but knew that I did. Secret collecting isn't the way to grow a collection. One friend was so well known for his hobby that he once received a letter addressed to "Mr. Postcard, Stevens Point, Wisconsin."

A good way to advertise your interest is to display them in libraries or schools, wherever there's a locked case. Local newspapers are often willing to feature town views from the early days and credit the collector. To avoid worry about theft, be sure to get a fine arts rider on your insurance. Waiting for treasure to come to you doesn't always pay off, at least not in the short run: those who find postcards are those who are looking for postcards.

Besides the obvious sources, shows, estate sales, and shops, I've found postcards at garage sales, church rummage sales (look in little bundles or boxes of stationery) and, of course, auctions. One small town auction was proudly displaying two albums of old postcards, but there was nothing special in either, mostly greetings that may have been a dealer's culls.

But since I was there, I poked around in all the boxes, including one pushed under a table. There was nothing but junk on top, but underneath was a virtual treasure trove of postcards mailed from East Germany in the Iron Curtain days. I bought the box for practically nothing, while others bought the albums for high prices. I took my treasure home, greatly pleased because the cards were franked with colorful DDR stamps, seldom found used on cover.

A network of traders is another way to strike postcard gold. Lucky collectors live near a postcard club with members willing to exchange, but it's also possible to make good trades with people who don't collect cards. I've traded books, photographs and paper dolls for post-

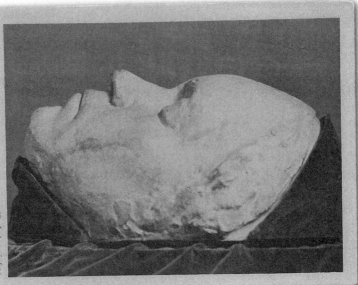

cards, sometimes to dealers.

If you're looking for a few special cards to fill out sets or series, let your favorite dealers know. But if a big bunch of postcards is your idea of treasure, enlist those close to you and always keep your eyes open for the unexpected.

INTEREST IN REAL PHOTO POSTCARDS, VINTAGE CHROMES PUSHES VALUES TO NEW HEIGHTS

Jefferson R. Burdick, a man of very modest means, left approximately 80,000 old postcards to the Metropolitan Museum of New York in 1963 as part of a much larger ephemera collection.

In the late 1970s, Russian Nikolai Tagrin claimed to have the world's largest postcard collection, more than 700,000, in his crowded Leningrad apartment where shelves filled with albums covered every wall.

Surprisingly, neither of these collections was the largest ever. One Czech collector was rumored to have several million, although confirmation of the card count in huge collections is impossible.

Others, including at least one in the United States, claimed to have a million.

If this sounds like a numbers game, it was. In the first half of the 20th century, postcards were cheap, often 1 cent and rarely more than 5 cents on the racks. Worldwide exchanges were common, making it possible to gain huge variety without being rich.

Those days are gone forever, but collectors today are just as avid about their acquisitions.

What postcards are bestsellers today? The people most likely to have the pulse of the hobby are dealers who offer thousands of cards to the public every year.

Ron Millard, long-time owner of Cherryland Auctions and Mary L. Martin, known for running the largest store in the country devoted exclusively to postcards, have offered some insights into the current state of the market. Both dealers have taken a son into their business, a sure sign of the confidence they have in the future of postcard collecting.

Real photo postcards of the early 1900s are highly rated by both dealers. Mary Martin, who sells at shows as well as through her store, reports that interest in rare real photos is "increasing faster than they

No.154. Chinese Monkey Player.

can be bought."

Ron Millard, whose Cherryland Auctions feature 1,800 lots closing every five weeks, indicates that real photos seem to be "holding steady with prices actually rising among the lower-end real photos as some people shy from paying the huge prices they have been bringing … Children with toys and dolls have been increasing and also unidentified but interesting U.S. views."

Cherryland bidders have also been focused on "advertising cards, high-end art cards, Halloween, early political and baseball postcards." Movie stars, other famous people and transportation, especially autos and zeppelins also do very well. Lower priced cards with great potential for rising in value include linen restaurant advertising, "middle range" holidays, and World War I propaganda.

Millard also cites vintage chromes, especially advertising, "really starting to take off with many now bringing $10 to $15. (These were $1 cards a few years ago.)"

At one time, foreign cards were largely ignored by collectors, but online sales have broadened the international market. In Millard's experience, "the sky is the limit on any China related." A few months ago Cherryland had a huge influx of new bidders from Australia, and the number from Asia is also increasing.

Martin sees hometown views as the most popular category, with real photo social history, dressed animals and Halloween also in high demand. She reports: "We see a lot of interest in military right now, and I don't believe it has really peaked yet." Social history from the 1950s and '60s also does really well. She's encouraged by the number of new and younger collectors at postcard shows.

Will anyone want your postcards when you're ready to sell? It's a valid question, and our two experts have good advice for anyone with a sizeable accumulation, say 500 or more postcards.

Auctions are one good option, both for direct purchases and consignments. Millard is always looking for quality postcards to offer collectors worldwide. His firm can handle collections of any size from small specialized to giant accumulations and are willing to travel for large consignments. Active buying is a necessity for dealers to keep their customers supplied, which should reassure collectors that their cards will have a ready market. Contact Millard at cherrylandauctions@charter.net.

Martin suggests that collectors go back to some of the dealers who sold them cards when they're ready to sell. Her firm is always willing to buy back good quality cards. She also sees reputable auction houses as a good avenue, and strongly suggests: "They should never be sold as a very large group if they can be broken down into different subject matter or topics." Martin can be contacted at marymartinpostcards@gmail.com.

Both experts agree there's an active demand for quality collections. That would exclude postcards in poor condition, a caution for collectors expanding their holdings. Look for the best and pass up damaged and dirty cards.

Billions of postcards were produced in the last century on practically every topic imaginable. As collections become more specialized, new subjects are sure to attract attention.

Many outstanding collections were put together with moderate expense by people who were among the first to recognize the value of a new collecting area.

As an example of an area yet to be fully explored, the photographers who made postcards possible haven't been widely collected in their own right. Many were anonymous, but some, like Bob Petley, famous for Western views as well as comic humor, have attracted collectors' attention.

The Tucson Post Card Exchange Club has made a specialty of gathering and listing the output of their "favorite son." No doubt there are fresh, new specialties just waiting to be discovered.

Postcard collectors love history, appreciate fine art, enjoy humor, and above all, are imaginative. There's every indication that today's favorite topics will be joined by new and exciting ones in the future.

REAL PHOTOS MAKE FUN POSTCARDS

What does a photographer do when times are tough and competition is stiff? Those who survive use their imaginations and offer a little something extra. This is certainly what professionals did during the postcard craze of the early 1900s.

The beginning of the 20th century was an exciting time for photography. In 1884 George Eastman developed a method of developing dry gel on paper, replacing the need for bulky photographic plates.

In 1901 the Kodak Brownie camera was marketed to the public, ushering in a whole new era in photography. A year later the Eastman Kodak Company started marketing photographic paper formatted as postcards.

The real photo postcard was born.

Once the world of photography was open to anyone who could afford

a modest investment in a Brownie, professionals had to offer more than an ordinary snapshot or portrait. The imaginative result was a combination of art and photography on the easy-to-mail, now highly collectible postcard.

One gimmick was to offer a fanciful setting. The most popular was a moon with stars or clouds in the background. The client would sit on the moon, possibly made of wood since people actually seem to be supported on these uncomfortable perches. Who wouldn't want to send friends a postcard of the first man or woman on the moon? One "moon" card in my collection even shows two women with boxes of Jell-O, utilizing a clever idea as advertising.

A favorite device was to provide a painted or wooden figure with a hole for a real person's head. (I recently saw the same setup outdoors at a zoo.) Some early ones were painted on canvas with a place for the subject to stick his or her head. Others were more elaborate wooden figures based on the same idea. Fairs, expositions, and amusement parks often promoted the sale of souvenir photographic postcards using "stick-your-head-here" props, a practice that hasn't entirely died out.

A person didn't have to go to a studio or an amusement area to get a photo postcard that was a little out of the ordinary. Both professional and homemade photos could be developed with fancy borders or added artwork, making them a little more special. Artists drew flowers, leaves and natural features like trees and landscapes to provide eye-catching borders. The photographs were usually shown as an oval or a circle, although more fanciful shapes were used too.

Even ordinary stare-at-the-camera photos are fun to collect when the card is decorated in imaginative ways.

If the postcard was never mailed—and many weren't—the trade name is an aide to dating. Kodak's first advised stock paper had Velox printed in the stamp area. Azo was added in 1904. The Cyko marking belonged to the Ansco Company in the same era.

Prairie Fires and Paper Moons by Hal Morgan and Andreas Brown (1981) has a discussion of the dating and making of real photo post-cards in addition to many rare images. Serious collectors will want to find this benchmark book. It pretty much started the modern craze for old photo cards.

FANTASY VINTAGE POSTCARDS BRIGHTEN DRAB DAYS

Put your imagination in high gear, and there are some magical surprises waiting for you on vintage postcards. Before surreal art, before electronic games that take the player into strange new worlds, there were artists who created their own fantastical worlds on postcards. Those who collect greetings from the early 1900s most likely have a number of fantasy postcards already.

Rabbits dressed like humans, pumpkins running away from witches on brooms, and good old Santa all have strong elements of fantasy, but they're only a sampling of what's available in the magical world of artists' imaginations.

Fantasy art must have a magical or supernatural theme. Sometimes it's a new spin on an old myth or legend. Or an artist may create something new and fantastic based solely on his or her active imagination. Early postcard artists seem to especially enjoy taking something from nature and humanizing it. Mountains were given faces and personalities, frogs played banjos, pigs interacted with people, and cats were given distinctive personalities such as the somewhat sinister ones drawn by Louis Wain, a prolific postcard artist.

A special favorite of early postcard publishers was the moon, which lent itself to all kinds of faces. In fact, moon fantasy was so popular that many photo studies had big paper or wooden moons as

THE JERSEY DEVIL

JAN 1

Happy
New Year Greetings

With All Good Wishes.

" OF COURSE YOU CAN BRING NESSIE, SON

props for their work. Another but no less popular category involves mythical and legendary creatures. Cute little beings were more popular than huge and scary monsters, although both belong in a fantasy collection. Fairies, gnomes, brownies and elves are fairly easy to find on postcards, and more often than not, they're playful and cute.

Margaret W. Tarrant, a British artist born in 1892, drew especially charming fairies as well as scenes picturing animals involved in human activities. She was a book illustrator, and her work appeared on many vintage postcards published by The Medici Society beginning in the 1920s and continuing for many years.

Human beings played a big part on the fantasy postcards of the early 1900s. Sometimes people were given bizarre characteristics or put into imaginary situations through "trick" photography. Other cards were artist drawn, using human features in "magical ways." Favorite themes were pretty women's faces on flowers or the addition of butterfly wings. Babies – lots and lots of babies crowded onto one postcard – were also pictured to magical effect.

They appeared in birds' nests, hatching from chicken eggs, or huddled together by the dozens in impossible scenes. Transportation themes were popular too. Cars and outhouses flew, and people rode everything from flying fish to carts pulled by chickens. Postcards that fooled the eye are among the most popular fantasy themes. What appears to be a skull of a famous person might be composed of semi-nude women draped in writhing positions.

Fantasy postcards can be comical or creepy, beautiful or bizarre. They can be found among foreign cards, holiday greetings, artist-signed cards or comics. Some will be offered for a sizable price, especially if the seller appreciates their unique nature. Others can be found modestly priced. Perhaps only a sophisticated dealer will have a sizable category of fantasy postcards, but the chances are good that anyone with a reasonably large collection will already own an assortment of these entertaining and imaginative cards.

THE FAIRY TROUPE
by
Margaret W. Tarrant

No. 3012.
SERIES B.

Chimpanzee at Typewriter,
New York Zoological Park.

Copyright 1907 by the
New York Zoological Society.

ANIMAL WONDERLAND
ON POSTCARDS

A huge project is underway to catalog every one of the 1.8 million species on planet earth. According to a BBC News report, this huge Encyclopedia of Life now has 30,000 pages and is scheduled for completion in 2017. It will be a treasure trove of information on new, current, threatened, endangered and recently extinct species, a virtual who's who of life on earth that includes both the animal and plant kingdoms.

No one will ever have a postcard collection picturing all 1.8 million life forms. In fact, only a few rare collectors ever accumulate more than a million different postcards, let alone a million plant and animal cards, but the scope of this scientific project can serve as an inspiration to nature lovers/collectors.

There's no way to know how many postcards have been produced

(109) DOTTED-FINNED PARROTFISH (*Scarus punctulatus*)

picturing different species, but animals, in particular, have been favorites for more than a hundred years. Raphael Tuck, an early British publisher whose name is well known to collectors, was a pioneer in issuing animal studies in sets, but some of the most interesting came from zoos and museums.

The New York Zoological Society was particularly clever in the cards it issued to sell to visitors and promote the Zoological Park. Two good examples are zookeepers handling an especially long snake and bored chimps wearing keepers' uniforms. Early ones date to 1907.

Zoos across the U.S. and in foreign countries tapped into the public's interest in animal life, although cards from some smaller zoos show big animals like bears in small cages that would be considered cruel today. Private and tourist-orientated animal displays were also prolific producers of postcards. It's a rare collector who hasn't run across a card from an alligator farm. They were popular attractions from Florida to California, two states also known for ostrich farms.

Museums used a more scientific approach, also including information on the backs of postcards. Unlike zoos, their exhibits were stuffed, often in backgrounds depicting the natural habitant.

The National Wildlife Society, pioneers in conservation efforts, published some very attractive matt finish artist-drawn wildlife scenes in the 1930s. Some collectors have also made an effort to collect all the state birds drawn by Ken Haag in the 1960s. Others prefer more fanciful cards like the dressed cats published by Max Kunzli of Zurich.

Not all animal cards are pleasant. It's hard to enjoy a 1913 real photo showing a whale being cut up or the reproduction of a scene where a school of 1500 "black fish," washed up on the beach and died in1884 at South Wellfleet, Mass. The dead whales sold for $15,000, divided among 300 inhabitants.

Collectors tend to specialize in one or a few animals. Elephants are popular with good reason. They're apt to be one of the first exotic animals a child sees. I can remember riding on one at a Chicago zoo even before I started school. Bears are favorites, and the antics of chimps never cease to amaze. Some prefer more cuddly creatures like domestic cats and dogs, and birds offer immense variety. It's hard to resist a beautiful racehorse or a more lumbering beast of burden.

Animal life is plentiful on cards from the early 1900s to the present, with many beautiful wildlife scenes from Alaska to exotic "Z" countries in Africa. The huge effort going into the Encyclopedia of Life may inspire some nature lovers to see just how many different species can be collected on postcards. It would also be a wonderful way to introduce children to collecting, especially if they have an interest in science.

Postcard publishers, artists and photographers have put the natural world within reach of all collectors. At a time when many postcards have become too expensive for the budget-conscious, there's unlimited potential at modest cost for those who want to admire and learn more about the species that inhabit our earth.

WISHLIST FOR A PERFECT POSTCARD

Every collector has a different idea of what the perfect postcard is.

Some might favor a particularly beautiful card, perhaps one by an Art Nouveau artist. Others look for the historical importance of a real photo or a bargain on a very valuable card. For those who collect complete series, a particularly scarce card needed for completion would rank highest. A collector can also be motivated by sentiment or nostalgia, particularly drawn to a significant scene or event remembered from childhood. In fact, there are probably as many ideas of what the perfect postcard should be as there are collectors.

Two things that any "perfect" postcard should have are scarcity and excellent condition. It goes without saying that a common card that can be found almost anywhere doesn't qualify. If three or four dealers at a postcard show have the same card for sale, it's not special enough to be on most collectors' wish lists.

Everyone has an individual standard for condition. Some will overlook minor flaws if the card warrants it. Others will hold out for an example without any visible faults. But virtually no one wants a soiled, foxed, ill-smelling card with missing corners, bends, tape-marks or pinholes. I particularly dislike rotted bits of rubber band adhering to either side of the card, ink smears, crayon marks and cancellation stains that mar the picture side. Cracked gelatin surfaces on old greeting cards are also a turnoff, as are postcards with food stains or marks from being used as a coaster.

For years I collected anything that took my fancy, but recently my quest for the perfect postcard has become more specific. First of all, I want a card that's been used at its point of origin. That means that the postmark must match the view. It should be a sharp strike that gives both the town and the state, plus the full date. Pre-1930 cards are preferable, as are hand strikes (as opposed to machine cancels), although this isn't a deal-breaker.

Small towns are definitely more interesting than larger ones, meeting the

View Showing State Bank Bldg & Interurban Station

Colon Mich

Public School

MAIN ST. LOOKING WEST LEHI UTAH

scarcity criteria. I tend to collect any decent view if the postmark is good, but main street scenes top my list. If the card is a real photo, all the better. Real photo street scenes vary from dark, smudgy views of empty streets to wonderful "slices of life" with people, transportation, interesting storefronts and signs. Two of my favorites show a banner for a women's suffrage meeting and damage after Halloween, but neither meets the cancellation criteria.

Unfortunately some postcards have been ravaged by stamp collectors. A "perfect" small town card with a matching cancellation should also have the stamp intact, even if it's a common stamp. It harks back to condition. There's something particularly unsightly about a glue stain where the stamp was steamed off.

Then there's location. Good examples from the Eastern Seaboard states are relatively easy to find, and the Midwest yields a fair number. But go farther west, and cards that meet all the above criteria get much scarcer.

Since this is about the search for the perfect postcard, it's all right to be even more demanding. It adds to the postal aspects if there are cancellations from both the point of origin and the receiving town or if the postal service added other markings. Then there stamps that are seldom seen on postcards. Think parcel post, airmail, special delivery or commemorative stamps. Sometimes both an American and a foreign stamp are used on the same card, or a foreign stamp has an American cancellation.

In my whole collection, I only have one card franked with a stamp from the 1893 Chicago Columbian Exposition, and that's a later greeting. Imagine what a prize a stamped postcard from the expo would be. Another real treasure is an early Christmas seal tied onto a card by having part of the cancellation touching it.

An interesting message is a plus too, especially if it sheds light on everyday happenings in the life of a sender. And the ultimate special feature would be association with a well-known person. I have a few postcards autographed by famous people and one addressed to an entertainer, but they fall short in the town/cancel combination.

Needless to say, I've never found a "perfect" postcard that incorporates all the above features, but those that come close give an intense feeling of holding history in my hands.

FAIRY TALE POSTCARDS
CHARM COLLECTORS

Once upon a time in a faraway kingdom, a beautiful princess was rescued by a heroic (and of course, handsome) prince with a little magical help, while an evil stepmother (witch, wizard or whatever) was suitably punished.

If I hadn't visited this mystical land many times as a child, it's unlikely I would have made a career of writing romance novels. In spite of decades of evidence to the contrary, part of me still believes in fairy tales and happy endings.

The essence of fairy tales is that they take place in an imaginary land, but the stories themselves are usually lacking in descriptive details. A castle is a castle. It comes with towers, a throne room and dungeons as required by the tale, but only the details necessary to the story are given.

H. C. Anderſen   Der Schweinehirt   O. Herrfurth pinx.

Perhaps this is because fairy tales have been inherited by children who have little patience with wordiness. Originally, almost every culture known to man had its magical tales peopled with fairies, elves, witches, giants, talking animals and all manner of mythical creatures, not to mention heroes and heroines.

They were heard and passed on by adults by word of mouth.

When the Brothers Grimm started gathering märchen, German tales, they couldn't have predicted that this type of story would become a staple of children's literature for many, many generations to come.

Fortunately, book publishers and artists created magical settings of their own to compliment fairy tales (which need not have fairies), adding greatly to the rich tradition. Collectors also benefit greatly from the visual portrayals, since artistic fairy tale scenes were reproduced on postcards beginning in the early 1900s.

A list of those who created fairy tale art includes many famous names: Walter Crane, George Cruikshank, Maxfield Parrish, Gustave Doré, Arthur Rackham and many others. Postcard collectors will also recognize these names: Mabel Lucie Attwell, Ivan Bilibine, Jessie Wilcox, Oskar Herrfurth, Margaret Tarrant.

Raphael Tuck & Sons published one of the earliest fairy tale series, attractive embossed cards embellished with gold. They have undivided backs, which unfortunately allowed a message on the front side only, a drawback in collecting the earliest used cards. The series numbers, 3471 ff, are printed on the picture side along the right edge, unlike later Tuck series numbered on the address side.

The examples in my collection were used in 1902. Around the same time, Tuck also used a lovely Sleeping Beauty scene on a Christmas card. O. Herrfurth was the artist on some particularly nice German series that tell a story in pictures. His postcards most commonly seen in this country are "The Swineherd," by Hans Christian Andersen, "The Pied Piper of Hameln" (the Rattenfnger or rat exterminator in Hamelin), and "The Surprising Adventures of Baron Munchausen" (a collection of tall tales), all of which I found for sale on eBay.

For collectors who don't limit themselves to well-known artists, fairy tale themes show up both in story book series and on greetings. An artist named Kirchbach signed some attractive foreign cards for traditional favorites such as "Sleeping Beauty" and "The Princess and the Pea."

In recent years, folklorists have examined fairy tales to explain ancient customs, and historians have tried to trace their origins. Psychologists try to explain underlying themes according to their discipline, but do we really want to know that magical tales were all about adolescents finding themselves?

Fairy tales are a rich heritage, first introduced in childhood and nurtured by astonishing art. A single postcard scene can open up this imaginary world. A collection can transport the viewer to a kingdom where good triumphs and the princess lives happily ever after with her hero.

SILHOUETTE PROFILE PORTRAITS

Taste in art changes just as surely as swings in fashion, so it's not surprising that the craze for late Victorian postcards had drastically diminished by the end of World War I. Art Deco came onto the scene as a refreshing change from the elaborate, often stylized designs of the early 1900s. In this country, the use of postcards as holiday greeting gradually shrank to practically nothing, replaced by cards mailed in envelopes.

In Europe, an old art form, the silhouette, was revived in the years between the two world wars in the spirit of Art Deco. Creative artists gave it new life with sprightly designs and the addition of colorful details.

Postcards were illustrated with charming silhouettes that seemed delightfully fresh and original at the time. The name for this art comes from Etienne de Silhouette (1709-1767), the French finance minister under Louis XV. He amused himself and others with cutout portraits in black that eventually took his name. He was so famous for his stinginess that "Silhouette" was used to mean "cheap," and it was a very inexpensive method of creating a likeness.

Silhouettes, or "shades" as the English called them, grew in popularity until they were eventually replaced by photography.

A silhouette can be made by cutting the image from paper, traditionally black, and pasting it on a background sheet, or by drawing an outline and filling it in with India ink or other solid color. The ancestors of silhouette art go back to classical times in the black figures decorating Greek vases.

Profile portraits were very popular in the United States in the 19th century. For a very small fee compared to painting in oils, a silhouette artist could provide a decorative memento of a loved one.

By the early 1900s when postcards were a major fad, it was still possible to find artists who could cut a silhouette portrait. The most desirable American silhouette postcards have small cut-outs of real people pasted on them, most probably made quickly at fairs or other events.

American publishers also put out some humorous silhouettes, but for the most part, they were rather crude and never became big sellers. It does seem that postcard makers missed an opportunity in the 1920s and '30s because silhouettes found a ready home in the magazines and books of the day. The famous silhouettes of Nancy Drew and her sleuthing friends that appeared on the end papers of the mystery series for girls are so appealing that they're still being reproduced today. In fact, a friend sent me a note last week on stationery decorated with them.

Silhouette postcards are mostly European. A number of talented artists worked in this medium, either cutting or drawing them and sometimes adding touches of color. Many that are collected today originated as book illustrations and were reproduced on postcards. The artists' names are gradually becoming familiar to American collectors as they appear on auction lists or in dealers' stock. Among the noteworthy are Allmayer, Beckmann, Diefenbachs, Grosze, Kaskeline and Plilschke, to name only a few. Many postcards are available for $10 to $15 in excellent condition, a very reasonable range considering the quality and appeal of the art.

METAMORPHIC POSTCARDS FOOL THE EYE

There's been a barrage of allegedly-true television shows on ghosts, demons, aliens, UFO's and mysterious creatures like the Loch Ness monster. In almost every case, the main proof for the existence of these supernatural beings comes from eyewitness accounts. The skeptical among us can only turn to a basic scientific question: How does the brain process what the eye registers? Do we always see what we think we're seeing?

Artists recognized the quirky nature of human vision many centuries ago, inventing a technique called trompe-l'oeil (French for "trick-the-eye"). Basically it's an optical illusion that makes a two-dimensional painted object seem real. Greeks and Romans used it in murals, and the technique became especially popular in the Renaissance and Baroque periods. It could be architectural, such as putting in a door or window and fooling the viewer into believing it was real, but sometimes it was done for fun.

Imagine a fly on a picture frame or a character trying to climb out of the painting. The metamorphic postcards of the early 1900s used a playful technique that is as entertaining today as it was then. Basically, an image is transformed before the viewer. What appears as a human head, skull, or other realistic image challenges the perception. Scrutinized from a different angle or up close, it becomes a collection of smaller objects. For example a Satyr, a mythical creature, is made up of women positioned and posed in the shape of a face.

The name "metamorphic" is used for this type of postcard because a "metamorphosis" is a striking alteration of form or appearance. No one person has been credited with this type of postcard art, although an artist named Volz is credited with a print picturing Napoleon in the style.

Postcards are an especially effective way to present metamorphic art, basically because they're small. On a large print, the "trick" would be too obvious. Viewers would instantly see that the whole is composed of separate images. It is much easier to deceive the eye if the picture itself is diminutive. Much of the fun is derived from a close look at the composition of the whole.

Metamorphic postcards frequently were designed as caricatures of the famous. They picture people whose faces were familiar to those living in the early 20th century. Some visages, like Beethoven's and Napoleon's, are well known today. Others, although their names are remembered, may not be as easy to identify. People like Schiller (German historian, playwright and poet) and Wagner (composer and favorite of Hitler) left their mark on history but their faces are largely forgotten. Others like Bismarck (German leader), Wilhelm II (German Kaiser during WWI), and Franz Joseph I (Austrian emperor) show up in history books, but many people might not recognize their pictures. A collection of metamorphic postcards can appeal to history enthusiasts, although they are probably collected more because the artwork is fun.

There's a good variety of metamorphics available. Skulls and devil heads were popular, as were mythical creatures like the faun. Some show that they were made in Europe, while others give no written indication of their origin, perhaps because they were pirated. They're generally offered at prices beginning around $25, although higher prices are justified for the rarer examples. Some use normal portraits and hide figures within them, like the puzzles that challenge children to find hidden objects in a picture. If these aren't, strictly speaking, metamorphic, they do add to the pleasure of a collection.

Even though most metamorphic postcards are around 100 years old, they still intrigue viewers with the question: Am I seeing what I think I'm seeing? Eyes can be fooled, but illusion can be fun.

Napoleon was a favorite for caricatures, and there are also metamorphic postcards showing a front view of his face. This one was almost certainly published in the United States, but there isn't any way to identify the maker, possibly because it was an unauthorized copy of a French postcard. It's dark green with a postcard logo widely used before 1915. Unlike more risque art using scantily clad women, this card uses heroic images. Napoleon's nose is a horse's head, and his lips are the hat or helmet of the man who forms his chin. His eye is the head of the cavalry soldier who rides his nose. A careful look shows that his collar is a seated military man, and mounted men ride across his hat. Some details were drawn in, such as hair and eyebrows, while others are not distinct.

CHAPTER 2

PEOPLE ON POSTCARDS

CELEBRATE CHARLES DICKENS WITH ANTIQUE POSTCARDS

Charles Dickens terrified me.

We first crossed paths when I was 5, visiting my grandparents in Saginaw, Mich. A neighbor invited us to hear a recording of *A Christmas Carol.* I sat mesmerized by clanking chains and ghostly voices. They seemed to follow me to the big room with the closet where I slept

alone in a bed with a ceiling-high carved headboard.

Dickens introduced me to fear. I recently reread *A Christmas Carol,* and it was every bit as chilling and engrossing, although I no longer expect spooks to come out of my grandmother's big walk-in closet.

As an author, Dickens had the exceedingly rare ability to make his characters come alive. Kind-hearted, evil or morally ambiguous, they endure in some of the best novels ever written. He created them to inhabit a Victorian world of poverty and injustice, one he knew well.

Dickens' father was imprisoned for debt, along with all the family members except Charles, who was sent to paste labels on boxes in a shoe-blacking factory. *David Copperfield*, his most autobiographical novel, gets its realism from his own experiences.

Feb. 7, 2012 was a big day for admirers of Dickens: it was the 200th anniversary of his birth in 1812. Very few novels are popular after the death of their authors. An exceedingly small number become "great" literature, but almost no one would deny that Dickens deserves his place in literary history. He wrote page-turners with humor, heart and pathos. My introduction to him was scary, but my grandmother's complete set of Dickens still has pride of place in my library.

As a postcard subject, Dickens is a rewarding challenge. By the early

Series of 12.   Published for the Pickwick "Leather Bottle," Cobham, Kent.   No. 1.

THE "LEATHER BOTTLE," COBHAM.

Mr. Tupman here sought retirement from the world, after the elopement of Miss Rachael Wardle with Mr. Alfred Jingle. Dickens enjoyed taking his friends to the "Leather Bottle," rendered famous by the "Pickwick Papers."

CHARACTERS from CHARLES DICKENS.

"MR. MICAWBER."
(David Copperfield)

I am, however delighted
to add that I have now
an immediate prospect of
something turning up.

Kyd.

THE PICKWICK PAPERS

In Dickens Land

"Wot I like in that 'ere style of writin'," said the elder Mr. Weller, "is, that there ain't no callin' names in it—no Wenuses nor nothin' o' that kind. Wot's the good o' callin' a young ooman a Wenus or a angel, Sammy?" —Chapter xxxiii.

1900s, he was a national icon in Britain and appeared in many highly collectible sets. *The American Postcard Guide to Tuck* by Sally Carver (1976) was the first to call attention in the U.S. to the six-card sets designed by notable postcard artists. She lists eight series, including three with character sketches and three "In Dickens Land," featuring scenes from his novels. KYD and Harold Copping signed some.

Tuck's series were typically sold in sets of six, protected by illustrated envelopes. Raphael Tuck and Sons was the first postcard firm to cater to collectors, so these sets were often kept intact rather than being mailed. Even when the envelopes are worn, the cards tend to be in mint condition, something collectors love.

Tuck's sets are only the beginning of a Dickens collection. In the days before movie favorites and rock stars, authors had big followings. Dickens was often included in sets of famous writers, including an American one published by John Winsch in 1910.

Naturally, the home of such a famous author was destined to become a museum. Postcards picture the home where he lived and worked, as well as just about any place he was known to frequent. (You can still have a pint in one of his favorite London taverns.)

With the plenitude of celebrities vying for attention today, authors aren't showing up on postcards the way they were in the early 1900s, but it is possible to find later cards.

Recently I came across a series of silhouettes signed with the initials FES (or FEB, or FOG) — anyway, a series by an artist who needed penmanship lessons. No publisher is listed, but one card was mailed from England with a smudgy postmark and a stamp from the early 1950s.

Dickens endeared himself to Americans when he toured to give readings from his novels in 1842 (protesting slavery) and again in 1867 when he was plagued by poor health. He loved acting and played all the parts when he read from his works. He also performed in plays in Britain, deserting his wife — the mother of his 10 children — for an actress. (He was talented, not perfect.)

So, Charles Dickens, you're forgiven for frightening a child and remembered for your truly wonderful novels. Happy 200th birthday!

H.M. QUEEN ALEXANDRA

The Prince and Princess of Wales

ROYAL MANIA? A LOOK AT ROYALS ON POSTCARDS

The British royals are unique in their ability to grab headlines and generate excitement, especially for big events like births, anniversaries, coronations, birthdays, and above all, weddings. When an heir to the throne marries, it's superstar time. Prince William, Charles and Diana's handsome son, married his long-time girlfriend, Kate Middleton, on Friday, April 29, 2011, in Westminster Abbey. Every detail of the event from her dress to the problem of the black sheep uncle has been

rehashed in the media over and over and over again.

Every royal since Victoria's son, Edward VII (1901-1910), has been duly commemorated by postcard publishers, most commonly Raphael Tuck and Sons until their plant was destroyed in 1940.

People love souvenirs, and the British have always been eager to purchase everything sellers offered featuring their royals. Tourists, too, buy royalty postcards, so it seems probable that William and Kate cards were on the racks before the big event.

The press and the people had a long love affair with Princess Diana. Postcards issued for her wedding include a pair of all silver and another all gold commemorative cards along with countless pictures of the couple. In fact, there are so many of her blue outfit, it's a shame she didn't change between shots.

Prince Charles was in no hurry to take a bride, so there's a fairly long time span between his marriage in 1981 and his parents' in 1947.

In the austere days after World War II, the wedding of Elizabeth and Phillip was modest compared to the spectacle of their son's, but the young princess won the hearts of the nation by pitching in to help during the war. The public must have enjoyed seeing the man she was marrying on a nice set of photo postcards issued by Valentine's, a noteworthy British publisher.

If there were any postcards made for the marriage of Edward VIII and his American wife, the woman he renounced the throne for, I haven't seen them. The coronation of his brother, George VI, subject of the popular new film, "The King's Speech," was commemorated by a nice photographic postcard shown here.

As every postcard collector knows, the postcard craze began in the early 1900s and declined by the beginning of World War I. During the peak years, both the quantity and quality of postcards was astonishing. George V sat on the British throne from 1910 to 1936, so postcards from his reign aren't particularly scarce. Some, though, are very attractive, especially lithographed cards made in Germany, where most of Tuck's (and the world's) were printed. It was George V who changed the name of the royal family from Saxe-Coburg-Gotha to the House of

SOUVENIR OF CORONATION
OF THEIR MAJESTIES
KING GEORGE VI AND QUEEN ELIZABETH

H.M. THE KING.

H.M. THE QUEEN.

Windsor, reacting to the German xenophobia of the First World War.

For those who are interested in the whole history of British royalty, it's possible to see portraits of all the kings and queens. Tuck produced three series of 12 cards each, No. 614, 615, and 616, plus one card in 617. These cards are pretty pricey if they can be found in complete sets, but countless world-famous artists also painted the royals. Art reproductions from museums are relatively inexpensive, and some, especially those of the Tudors with their elaborate clothing, are hugely entertaining.

The days when Henry VIII could say "Off with her head," and have it happen are long gone, but interest in the British royals hasn't diminished. Today there are so many ways to get a look at Prince William and Kate, postcards are almost an afterthought, albeit one many will appreciate as they did with the Charles and Diana wedding.

POSTCARDS OFFER UNIQUE IMAGES OF NATIVE AMERICAN ARTISANS

Native American art was introduced to mainstream collectors through Indian trading posts, such as Indian Plaza in Gallup, N.M., which opened to take advantage of tourist traffic on Highway 66. The famous highway, completed in 1926, gave souvenir hunters the opportunity to buy the work of highly talented crafts people, many of whom are now recognized as outstanding artists.

For tourists who didn't choose to get in on the ground floor by collecting the art, there were many postcards featuring artists and their works. It's still possible to study and enjoy many types of Native American art through the large number of cards purchased and saved by travelers. Silver jewelry, such as squash-blossom necklaces and concho belts, were popular favorites in the Southwest.

Early silversmiths learned their craft from Spanish and Mexican examples in the mid-19th century, melting down pesos and American dollars to obtain the silver. Da-Pah (later known as James Dapah) was

NAVAJO INDIAN SILVERSMITH PLYING HIS TRADE   C-25

SEE OTHER SIDE

1A1436

A235   BEN STANLEY'S CAFE
HIWAY 66-SOUTH OF MIAMI, OKLAHOMA

a well-known Navajo artisan who appears in the 1930s. He was known for sand painting and silversmithing, and his work was sold in Gallup, N.M. He also exhibited his work on the East Coast. Da-Pah died in 1977 at the age of 82.

Another highly valued craft was weaving. Legend says that the Navajo learned it from Spider Woman, one of the Holy People of the Underworld — or from the Pueblos in mid-17th century.

One outstanding weaver, Elle of Ganado, was chosen to make a red, white and blue blanket and present it to President Theodore Roosevelt on a two-hour stop he made in Albuquerque in 1903. She became well known for this honor and for her excellent work, making her a popular subject for postcards.

Baskets were also popular with early tourists. The first baskets were attributed to First Man and First Woman and had ceremonial uses in the underworld. The colors used in this ancient craft were very significant, with black representing mountains and red related to clouds and darkness.

Postcards from both Eastern and Western tribes feature basket making. The most famous Native American artist is Maria Montoya Martinez (1881-1980) who perfected a black pottery that is highly sought by collectors today.

Inspired by broken bits of polished black Neolithic pottery found in the New Mexico desert, she developed a highly complex method for making black-on-black ceramics. Her husband, Julian, helped in the process, although at the time pottery making was considered women's work. Their fame grew, and postcards showing Maria alone and with her husband are fairly common. She won many awards and exhibited at world fairs, passing her skills on to family and tribal members.

Collecting the art of these early 20th century artisans is costly.

Pieces that once sold as tourist souvenirs now command tremendous respect. Fortunately, the best Native American work can be enjoyed on postcards. The cards showing these talented artists at work document their unique place in the art world. They're likely to become more valuable as more people are attracted to Native American art.

Heat up this Post Card with Hot Flat-Iron, gas jet or match (Don't burn it).

What are Fritz and Hans up to?

Copyright, 1906, by American Journal Examiner.

THE MISCHIEF-MAKERS

Our local super-store has one sad rack of postcards with little to tempt even the most avid collector. A hundred years ago the situation was vastly different. Almost every topic under the sun was depicted on postcards, but none appealed to the general buyer more than adorable children.

Children were depicted as angels, Kewpies, cupids, romantic couples and advertising icons. They represented ethnic groups and frolicked in holiday settings, but above all, they were cute and irresistible. Artists who could capture the charm of young people could actually make a living doing art for postcards.

In this country Ellen H. Clapsaddle was the most prolific but her competition would make up a who's who of postcard artists. Clapsaddle (who never had kids) and her peers saw children through rose-colored glasses. Their work can be compared to a professional portrait today with children dressed in their very best and bribed or cajoled into smiling for the photographer. The finished pictures never show tears, temper tantrums or peanut-butter stains.

At the other extreme some artists saw the dark side of children and

I don't like this kid, so back he goes under the gooseberry bush.

used it with comic genius. Foremost among them was Rudolph Dirks, a German immigrant who made cartoon history with his Katzenjammer Kids. He began his comic strip in Hearst's New York Journal in 1897, and it's still syndicated by King Features, making it the oldest comic strip in American history.

Hans and Fritz were rebels long before the turbulent uprisings of the 1960s. They constantly bedeviled authority in the form of Mama, the Captain (a shipwrecked sailor, not their father although he tried to rein them in) and the school head, the inspector.

A BOY IN SUMMER-TIME

"I bet they're jealous because they ain't boys, too."

Copyrighted 1905 for John T. McCutcheon. No. 14.

Dirks later left Hearst and did a new comic strip based on the same characters called "Hans and Fritz," then "The Captain and the Kids." But before he left, the American Journal Examiner issued a rather unique series of postcards featuring the antics of the boys. In order to get the joke, the card had to be held to heat, either an iron, a gas jet or a match. There's no record of how many little fingers got singed in the process, but it seems easier to find these cards with the hidden figure revealed.

Dirks didn't have a monopoly on bad boys, although he seems to be the only artist who worked exclusively with delinquents. John T. McCutcheon, a newspaper cartoonist for several Chicago newspapers including the *Tribune*, had work reproduced on postcards in 1905.

Although his newspaper work was essentially political, he was right on target in his postcard series, "A Boy in Summertime."

Fred Spurgin is another artist to check out when looking for young mischief-makers. He was a prolific British artist especially noted for his World War I patriotic postcards, but he knew his subjects when it came to kids.

The devilry of boys appealed to postcard artists more than little girls' mischief, possibly because they were mostly men remembering their own childhood pranks. Any number of comic cards feature kids in trouble, even though the topic isn't the main subject of the artists.

Twelvetrees sometimes depicted the mischievous side of children. (There were two Twelvetrees. Charles H. drew the Johnny Quack comic strip from 1909 to 1911. Charles R. drew chubby-cheeked kids, but so did Charles H.). Lawson Wood, best known for his monkey calendars, drew kids in trouble, while some downright nasty kids show up from time to time on live-model cards. A boy about to hit an obese man with a stick would be an example of this.

For those who think kids are a hoot, the search for mischief-makers promises nostalgia as well as fun.

REAL-LIFE HEROES ON POSTCARDS

Recognizing superheroes on postcards is easy. They sport bright tights and possess special powers. It's much harder to put together a collection of real life heroes, mainly because everyone's list of deserving people is different.

There are heroic leaders, military heroes, health heroes, explorers, adventurers and ordinary people who perform amazing feats of courage and

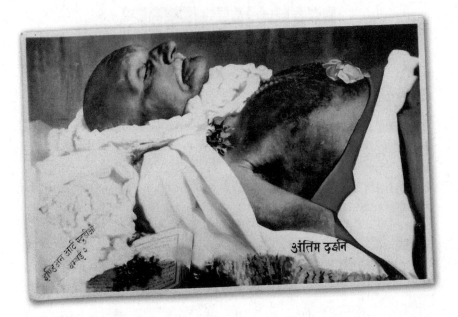

अंतिम दर्शन

self-sacrifice. (Note that "hero" as used here includes both genders.) As a postcard topic, real life heroes can be both illuminating and inspiring.

If postcard collectors have one thing in common, it's a desire to keep learning. The person who looks for hometown views constantly gathers new bits of information. The fan of artist-signed cards wants to know about the background of favorites. Ask anyone what he or she collects, and you'll find a person devoted to expanding knowledge as well as finding new images.

There are two ways to go in putting together a collection of real life heroes. The first is to look for famous people and decide later whether the person qualifies as a "hero." With information so easily available on the Internet and in public libraries, this can lead to some really interesting research.

Take Charles Lindbergh, for example. In 1927 he was credited with making the first non-stop solo flight from New York to Paris. The country went wild over their "hero," an aviator who had been working as an airmail pilot on the St. Louis-Chicago run. His triumph turned to

UNVAILING CUSTER MONUMENT MONROE MICH

tragedy when his infant son was kidnapped and murdered and the family retreated to Europe. His plane, the "Spirit of St. Louis," can still be seen at the Smithsonian.

Lindbergh postcards can be found without great difficulty, but it's an individual decision whether to include the flyer in a modern-day collection of heroes. (Check out his politics.)

A more focused approach is to make a list of most-admired people and choose one or a few as subjects in a comprehensive collection. Everyone's choices will be different. Presidents, war heroes and social activists like the early abolitionists are popular today. Yesterday's adventurers like the early polar explorers and the first astronauts have great appeal, but tracing more obscure heroes can be wonderfully challenging too.

For better or worse, I've always followed the first method: collect first, then see what I have. But even this hit-and-miss approach has helped me focus on a few most-admired heroes. As a child I had a lot of "pen pals." One in India sent me five memorial cards made after the death of Mahatma (the Great Soul) Gandhi in 1948, which I still consider among the most valuable in my collection.

Postcards relating to Martin Luther are relatively easy to find but invaluable when they lead to a study of his role in the Protestant Reformation. I augmented my Luther collection by creating a few maximum cards (postcard with related cancel and stamp) when the U.S. issued a stamp honoring him in 1983.

Jeanne d'Arc, the French peasant girl who led an army, is endlessly fascinating, and her life is well commemorated on French cards. Another woman who belongs in the hero (heroine) category is Florence Nightingale. Her postcards aren't common, even though she was the first to establish a training school for nurses – a lasting contribution to society.

Pick a real life hero, and endless possibilities open up. Besides portraits reproduced on postcards, there are birthplaces, relatives, statues, residences, monuments and cards related to accomplishments.

Biographies open endless possibilities. The best postcard of all would be one actually written by a hero. Finding an autographed one is a big thrill too. (I may have a genuine Jimmy Doolittle autograph on a postcard of his plane, but it hasn't been authenticated by an autograph expert.)

Real life heroes offer an engrossing way to collect, and better still, inspire our own lives.

SUPERHEROES ON SUPER POSTCARDS

As a child I read every comic book printed, but I never collected them in spite of my mania for accumulating everything from pebbles to paper napkins. No doubt some rare early issues went through my hands, but the deal with my dad was: Read and return.

He had a newsstand in his drug store and brought home one of each issue, then took them back to throw in a box with other unsold magazines that were returned to the distributor. It didn't make him popular with the news agency that had to sort them and tear off covers to receive credit, but it was all in the family. The manager married my aunt. (By the way, if you see piles of coverless books for sale today, they're stolen.)

No wonder I found Dick and Jane readers painfully dull! Who could

care whether Sally's cat climbed a tree after reading Batman or Superman's adventures? And, I have to confess, I've seen all the superhero movies as they come out.

It goes without saying that I jump at the chance to add superhero postcards to my collection. They're not terribly common, probably because copyright laws discourage unauthorized reproduction of the comic strip heroes, and they're not especially old either. Superman, the grand old man of incredible heroes, debuted 70 years ago, and the postcards I've gathered are considerably more recent.

A good beginning to a superhero collection is a set of Marvel Comics cards. They were obviously issued in book form, since one end of each card is perforated. Still a great find, they picture all the major Marvel heroes from the 1940s to the '70s. Captain America leads the way with his team, the Avengers. It includes some lesser-known characters such as Red Skull, an enemy sent against him by Hitler himself. In all, there are 32 cards in the set, including famous superheroes like Spider-Man, Captain Marvel, Ms Marvel (from the politically correct '60s), X-Men, Daredevil, Thor, his enemy Loki, and the Invaders, a team that helped fight World War II.

Superman is in a class by himself, and Metropolis, Ill., has claimed him as their favorite hometown boy. One continental size postcard shows the "Largest Superman Mural in the World." Another, with multiple views, shows a billboard painting of Superman, a painting on the town's water tower, a Superman award and Superman's only official phone booth. You almost expect him to be in front of the town hall handing out autographs. A few years ago DC comics issued a limited edition reproduction of the Superman #1 comic book. It came with a postcard of the historical cover that prompted me to buy a comic book for the first time since my children stopped reading them. For Batman fans, postcards copyright 1966 play into the popularity of the TV series with balloons of sometimes humorous dialogue. They were published by National Periodical Publications and printed by Dexter Press. I have Series #1, which has 10 cards. I don't know if other series were actually published, but here's a hint about Dexter Press cards. They tend to get cloudy or smudgy, but they can be restored with a light coat of gloss acrylic spray available in most craft stores. Follow directions on the can and practice on a common card first.

The U.S. Postal Service has issued series of stamps picturing superheroes and comic book covers. Finding (or creating) postcards franked with them can also make nice additions to a superhero collection.

Given their scarcity, superhero postcards are relatively inexpensive, but if the movies are any indication, they have great future potential.

JOSEPH V. STALIN   FRANKLIN DELANO ROOSEVELT   WINSTON SPENCER CHURCHILL

Three Great Leaders

THE RIGHT HONOURABLE SIR WINSTON CHURCHILL

WINSTON CHURCHILL: A STUDY IN GREATNESS

Does history create great leaders, or do great leaders shape history? Either way, postcard collectors can indulge their interest in history by pursuing links to one of the 20th century's foremost leaders and most colorful characters: Winston Leonard Spencer Churchill.

Famous people have long been a favorite topic on postcards, but few have the international appeal of the prime minister who led Britain during the dark days of World War II. He is a worthy subject to collect for that reason alone, but his whole life has levels of interest that suggest roles as unlikely as a modern-day King Arthur or a fictional Indiana Jones.

Churchill's life was complex from the beginning. His father, Lord Randolph Churchill, and his American mother, Jennie Jerome, might be accused of child neglect today, shipping him off to boarding school where he was a poor student handicapped with a speech impediment.

As a child of privilege, he became an army officer and served during the Boer War, but he "moonlighted" as a war correspondent to supplement his salary. His mastery of words brought him success as a writer of histories and eventually as a member of Parliament, although his first try in 1899 wasn't successful.

Churchill's character makes him fascinating. He was overly fond of alcohol and smelly cigars, and subject to what he called "the black dog," periods of deep depression that he weathered by painting landscapes. His verbal barbs were as clever as they were cutting.

Lady Astor, a native Virginian who became the first woman in Britain's parliament, once told him: "Winston, if I were your wife, I'd put poison in your coffee." His response: "Nancy, if I were your husband, I'd drink it."

Churchill served as prime minister from 1940 to 1945, when he was passed over for the peacetime job. He came back from 1951 to 1955, finally retiring because of failing health. He died in 1965 after a long marriage to Clementine Hozier. They were the parents of five children, one of whom died young.

The best approach to a collection of Churchill postcards is to begin with his photo portraits and World War II meetings with Roosevelt and Stalin then go on to document his long and varied career with its high and low points. Because he came from a long line of nobles, it's also possible to find portraits of his ancestors and ancestral homes.

The most important postcards honor Churchill's leadership during World War II. Sometimes it's subtle. For instance, postcards of the period sometimes had quotes of his on the back, even though the picture side wasn't related. For example, a Scottish scene of Alloway had this on the back:

"We shall continue steadfast in faith and duty till our task is done."

- The Prime Minister

His words were so much in the heart of his people that there was no need to include his name.

It's particularly fun to find Churchill in unexpected places. One is the Winston Churchill Memorial and Library in Fulton, Missouri. The remains of an English church built by Sir Christopher Wren in 1676 was moved to the campus of Westminster College. It was here that Churchill made his famous "iron curtain" speech.

Collecting postcards related to a famous person is most enjoyable when it becomes a learning experience. Begin with a good biography of Churchill, and there's no end of what his life teaches.

TRACKING SHERLOCK HOLMES ON POSTCARDS

When Arthur Conan Doyle grew tired of writing detective stories about Sherlock Holmes, he did what any sensible author would do — he killed him off.

The public was outraged when Holmes fell to his death over the Reichenbach Falls. Readers wept, mourned and made such an outcry that Doyle was shocked into reviving him. Today the brainy detective is probably the most famous fictional character in history.

Postcard collectors can identify with much that Holmes did. They love to search out clues to new finds, learning as they acquire.

And, let's be honest, they also seem a bit peculiar, as did the detective, to people who think a room full of postcards has no practical value.

Sherlock Holmes has been revived so many times in movies and on television that his name is familiar all over the world. Societies such as the Baker Street Irregulars (named after the street urchins who sometimes helped on his cases) and The Sherlock Holmes Society of London study his cases with intense interest. Visitors can visit his museum at 221 Baker Street.

But can an enthusiast put together a collection of Sherlock Holmes postcards? The answer is yes, certainly, but it requires the kind of doggedness that solved Holmes's most difficult cases.

The first Holmes story came out in 1887, "A Study in Scarlet," published in *Beeton's Christmas Annual*. *The Case-Book Of Sherlock Holmes* came out in 1927, marking the end of the fictional detective's career (Doyle died in 1930). This places the majority of cases in the late Victorian period, a time when the world was awash with postcards, the so-called "Golden Age" of the hobby.

So did Sherlock Holmes rock the postcard world the way he did the book world? I'm afraid not. The most desirable are reproductions of scenes drawn by Sidney Paget for *The Strand Magazine*. This artist produced 357 Holmes drawings, but only a few appear on older postcards and these aren't plentiful.

The easiest starting place for a Holmes collection is the internet. Modern postcards are fairly plentiful and include a Granada series featuring Jeremy Brett as Holmes in the TV productions. Another nice series was issued by the Royal Mail in 1993 picturing their five stamps honoring the detective.

Tracing the actors who played Holmes can lead to postcards. The oldest card in my collection shows the Baldwin Theatre in Springfield, Mo.

With a huge billboard announcing "Sherlock Holmes" by William Gillette, the actor most associated with the detective in this country. It was mailed in 1905.

For collectors who are up for a real challenge and enjoy reading his cases, there's another way to put together a Holmes collection. Doyle used real places in his stories, and in the early 1900 s postcard production was so great that it literally covered the world. Imagine how much it would add to the adventures of Holmes and Watson if the reader had an album of postcards showing all the places they went.

For those who already have a collection of London postcards, focusing on Sherlock Holmes can make it much more meaningful. Names like Pall Mall, Regent Circus, Brixton Road and Covert Garden Market will come alive in rereading the stories. Of course, Holmes traveled for cases, but how many people can imagine Aldershot or Wallington as it was in his day? Or Reichenbach Falls, the scene of his supposed death?

Holmes traveled by cab (horse-drawn) and train. Can you picture them in your mind? Did people really wear deerstalker hats? What about the coppers of the day? There's evidence in postcards!

Read the stories, make note of the settings and begin a search for the places where Sherlock Holmes did his crime fighting. It's a challenge worthy of the master detective.

FIRST LADIES ON POSTCARDS

Can a man do the First Lady's job? It is, after all, the most important unpaid position in the country. The requirements include being an excellent public speaker without contradicting the president, hosting parties that include a sea of unfamiliar faces with unpronounceable names, standing for hours in heels without shrieking in agony and shaking hands until your own is numb. It's also helpful to have a cause that the entire country supports and a wardrobe that won't make any worst-dressed lists.

Oh yes, there's also the gigantic task of insuring domestic harmony with a Type A politician and never, ever doing anything that provides fodder for the tabloids. Any man seeking the position might do well to take a good look at England's Prince Phillip. He's walked three steps behind his wife for over half a century, and no one has ever accused

DRESS OF SARAH CHILDRESS POLK

U. S. NATIONAL MUSEUM, SMITHSONIAN INSTITUTIO

ELEANOR ROOSEVELT

FIRST LADY OF THE W

HYDE PARK, NY
OCT
11
1984
12538

FIRST DAY ISSUE

him of being good-natured, sweet-tempered or pleasant. Whether our next first spouse is male or female, he or she will join an exclusive club of those who also served, sometimes with great distinction.

A friend in Texas recently sent me a postcard showing the rather shabby building that held the business of T.J. Taylor, a "dealer in everything" in Piney Woods. He was the father of Lady Bird Johnson, and my friend also sent an article from the Longview News-Journal about the first lady's early life. Her mother died when she was only 5, and her father wasn't up to the responsibility of raising a young child. She was sent to live with an unmarried aunt. It was a lonely life, but she did learn to love nature and books.

The big appeal of collecting First Lady postcards is the fascination of their life stories. Some were powerful, dynamic women; others came to the White House unprepared for the a public role, but almost all of them rose to the occasion.

Their individual backgrounds are as different as the men who served as national leaders. In the 20th and 21st centuries, they've all been wives, but six earlier presidents had to call upon a friend or relative to serve as official hostess.

Some First Ladies are unforgettable. Martha Washington is remembered as the first, and Dolly Madison's heroism is legendary for saving precious paintings before the White House was burned by the British. Eleanor Roosevelt has been honored internationally as a great humanitarian, and Betty Ford changed the way addictions are seen and treated. Jacqueline Kennedy made a huge splash as a trendsetter, and poor Mary Lincoln was probably driven insane by the deaths of her sons.

Postcards relating to these ladies are plentiful, but others are nearly impossible to find. Only the most avid historian knows much about Elizabeth Monroe, Jane Pierce or Helen Taft.

Fortunately, the Smithsonian has aggressively preserved the history and artifacts of all the First Ladies, displaying them in Washington, D.C., and more recently in a traveling exhibition. For many years the inaugural gowns were on display in a single room, and Smithsonian postcards are the best source for a complete collection of First Lady cards.

Early First Ladies are known mostly by their portraits, many painted by leading artists. More recently, First Ladies often took an active part in their husbands' campaigns and appear on postcards with them.

The serious collector will want to trace their lives through their birthplaces. A good example is the little house in Boone, Iowa, where Mamie Doud Eisenhower was born in 1896. It's now a small museum and a great source of town pride. Presidential libraries are also a source of First Lady postcards. There are many collectors of presidential postcards, and it's possible to assemble a huge collection. First Lady cards are much less plentiful, making the topic more challenging for those who enjoy researching and hunting for related cards. Generally speaking, it's not an expensive topic, but it is an open-ended one. There's always the promise of a new spouse in the White House.

MOVIE STARS ON POSTCARDS

From the editors of Antique Trader

When American movies began, there were no movie stars. In the early 1900s during the Nickelodeon era it was almost impossible to get stage actors and actresses to work in the movies. Salaries were a mere $5-$10 a day and there was no prestige. New York City financiers controlled the industry and they made huge profits casting unknown people who used stage names. Even travel expenses were limited. Fort Lee, N.J., was the site of western filming while dramas were filmed in the Bronx, Brooklyn or downtown Manhattan.

The audience at that time was made up of mostly immigrants who didn't mind the lack of sound at all. The dark movie theatre allowed them to escape their problems, including their inability to speak English, for a few hours. For the sum of one nickel they could engage in their fantasies, which was why films at that time all had a happy ending. But even these viewers began to identify with the cast. Letters arrived at studios addressed to "the man with the sad eyes" and similar salutations. This caused alarm among studio executives who were valiantly trying to control the production of films. If actors and actresses learned that some among them were receiving lots of letters from the public, he or she would surely demand more money. And, after all, movies were all about profits.

Another worry was D. W. Griffith, an actor who wanted to go into production. In 1908 he began to direct films for Biograph. Griffith experimented with ways to break the old rules. Through trial and error, he learned how to make the camera move and how to edit film. Most significantly, he kept moving his cameras closer to the faces of the performers. He quickly discovered that flat, harsh lighting and unsophisticated film was cruel to aging performers who did not want to use his new methods of performing. He needed youthful, unwrinkled performers who were not set in their ways. This set the stage for the emergence of beautiful people – the young and the very attractive.

Attendance at movies had expanded to include all Americans, and the public had begun to find out the identities of the people they saw on the screen, despite the best efforts of the studios to keep them secret. Flamboyant German-born Carl Laemmle created the Laemmle Film Service, which was the first independent film distribution company, to supply his chain of movie theaters. The major studios boycotted his distribution company so he started producing his own films through Independent

Motion Pictures (IMP) in New York. Laemmle is credited with creating the concept of a movie star – a specific young and beautiful performer that the audience expected to see on the screen regularly. Ironically, Laemmle was very concerned that the faces of his performers be recognizable but felt that their real names should be kept from the public. He hired Florence Lawrence for $1,000 a week but referred to her only as the "IMP Girl."

However, both the public and the star would not allow the face of Miss Lawrence to remain nameless. She and Mary Pickford moved on from IMP, and began making public appearances in their real names to promote their films. Laemmle also had bigger and better things in his future. He formed Universal Studios in Los Angeles in 1912, where he reigned until 1936. The movie stars gave stability to the mass production era that was now taking place in the film industry. Large numbers of viewers saw themselves, or at least a fantasy of himself or herself, by identifying with screen stars like Valentino or Barrymore or Garbo.

The movie stars between 1910 and the 1920s were probably unaware of the common chord they sounded within the American people. Yet they were the models for hundreds of stars to follow. The life of a movie star became a tangled web of reality and fantasy. Movie magazines appeared and they whetted the public's appetite for details about stars' personal lives. One of the most exciting things to know was where a favorite star lived.

At this same time in America, postcard collecting was a very popular hobby. Linen postcards picturing the stars and their homes were issued during the 1930s through the 1950s, and were popular with both postcard collectors and movie buffs. By the late 1950s hot television stars put movie stars on the back burner and this type of postcard was no longer issued. The high prices commanded by many movie collectibles, such as costumes and posters, make them too expensive for many movie enthusiasts. Available today for only $1-$2 each, postcards of movie stars' homes are an affordable collectible to remember a glamorous era.

CHAPTER 3

HOLIDAYS AND HAPPENINGS

CELEBRATE PRESIDENT'S DAY WITH VINTAGE GEORGE WASHINGTON POSTCARDS

Does anyone celebrate President's Day? There's something so bland about the made-up holiday that it must pass most people without a flicker of interest.

A century ago, George Washington's birthday was a red-letter date. He was born in Virginia on Feb. 22, 1732, and grew up pursuing his interests in western expansion and the military. He gained experience in the British army, participating in early skirmishes in what became the French and Indian War. In 1759, he settled down with his wife, Martha, to manage his lands at Mount Vernon and serve in the Virginia House of Burgesses. In 1775, he managed to get himself appointed command-er-in-chief of the Continental Army. The rest is familiar history.

An impressive number of postcards were made and sold to celebrate his life and his birthday — so many that they're still fairly easy to find.

WASHINGTON TAKING COMMAND
OF THE ARMY.

At a time when his portrait hung in most of the schoolrooms in the country, it's not surprising that postcard publishers promoted and sold a great many Washington cards, possibly more than for the Fourth of July and Memorial Day combined, if their availability today is any indication.

James Lowe's *Standard Postcard Catalog* (2nd ed. 1982) lists 42 different sets and series of Washington postcards, many of them published by Rafael Tuck and Sons. Although there's a certain irony that a British firm was the leading publisher of Washington postcards, it's not surprising. Tuck was the foremost international postcard publisher throughout the "Golden Age." Today Tuck's cards from the early 1900s are still among the most valuable and sought-after postcards.

The postmarks on Washington cards show that they were used to commemorate his birthday, not just for collectors of the day to tuck away in their albums. Most were mailed on the 20th or 21st of February, recalling a time when mail moved fast enough to arrive on the 22nd.

Tuck's postcards are especially nice to collect because they were

issued in numbered sets, something collectors appreciate when trying to find complete runs. Those that show Washington in scenes from history are eye-catching, but there is one caution when buying them sight unseen. They weren't always printed on the strongest card stock, so it's important that they are in excellent condition.

Washington cards were made by a who's who of important early publishers, including International Art, E. Nash and Illustrated Post Card. There aren't a great many signed artists, the exceptions being Ellen H. Clapsaddle and R. Veenfleit. George Washington postcards are especially noteworthy for their patriotic themes and the honor they pay to our first president.

To quote Gen. Henry Lee of Virginia, whose quote is on one card, Washington was: "First in war, first in peace, and first in the hearts of his countrymen."

MARDI GRAS LIVES ON

New Orleans didn't invent the Mardi Gras carnival, but the Louisiana city has given it such a unique heritage that the whole country must have sighed with relief to learn that it was held in 2006 in spite of hurricane damage.

As almost everyone knows, Mardi Gras means "fat Tuesday," the last day before Lent. In the Middle Ages, the French had a custom of using up all the fats in the home because it was a religious duty to abstain from meat. The church wanted to wean Christians from pagan celebrations held in February, so they changed them to Carnival, literally a "farewell to flesh."

Memories of Carnival inspired French-Canadian explorer Pierre le Monye to name Mardi Gras Point —on the Mississippi River 60 miles from New Orleans — in 1699.

French settlers in that city held masked balls to mark Carnival as early as 1718 until the Spanish banned them. When the Americans took over the city in 1827, the right to party in masks was restored, and Mardi Gras as it's known today was born.

The first official parade was held in 1837 with marchers in costume throwing sugarcoated peanuts to the crowd. The first float appeared in 1839 pulled by mules. Things got rowdy by the 1850s, so a secret society called the Mystick Krewe of Comus was formed to plan and organize the celebration. Since then, many societies have been involved.

In 1872, the Krewe of Rex was formed so the people of New Orleans had royalty to welcome the Grand Duke of Russia to the celebration. In 1909, the blacks of the city had their own parade with King Zula mocking the exclusivity of Rex and the white societies.

Mardi Gras has had its share of setbacks, including a collapsed balcony that killed people in the 19th century, and unruly behavior in the streets that caused controversy. It was canceled during the Civil War and both world wars.

Given its long and colorful history, it's not surprising that postcards documented the celebration throughout the 20th century. Most were made to be sold in the city as souvenirs of Mardi Gras and its colorful parades. Many well-known publishers of the pre-World War I-era produced scenes that are gems today and abundant enough to be available at reasonable prices.

WOMEN RIDICULED ON LEAP YEAR POSTCARDS

Women were threatening in 1908. They'd been in the forefront of the abolition movement before the Civil War, and they had saloons in their sights in the new century. Not only that, a dedicated few were agitating for the vote, a cause with growing support.

1908 was also the height of the postcard craze. A ride to the end of a trolley line was cause enough to send a card, and across the nation people were filling album after album with gorgeous, clever, witty and interesting postcards. It was no wonder that many publishers took a chance on a line of cards for Leap Year even though there would be no market for leftovers the following year.

At first glance, the connection between women's suffrage and Leap Year postcards may seem tenuous, but women's demand for the vote was getting serious by 1908. In 1890 Wyoming had become the first state admitted to the union with women's suffrage, followed by Colorado in 1893 and Utah in 1895. In Britain suffragettes began their campaign in earnest, storming the House of Commons that year.

What was the response of the average male? Ridicule! Some equated it with china painting and needlework, a female activity that would pass away when the ladies got bored. Others were threatened. If women got the vote, the fabric of (male) society would be shredded.

Leap Year postcards came on the scene in 1904, but the output that year was small compared to the hundreds of different designs issued in 1908 and 1912.

The main theme of Leap Year goes back to the folk tradition that women could propose marriage in that year. Some look back to St. Patrick in the 5th century as the beginning of this role reversal. A 13th-century legend says that if a man refused a Leap Year proposal, he had to give compensation in the form of a gift to the spurned woman. A whole year of this could be wildly expensive, so it was limited to one day only, Feb. 29. Whatever the origin, the postcard artists of the early 1900s ran with it. The Leap Year theme became woman's hapless quest for a marriageable man. Women were pictured trying to catch a man with a butterfly net, a pistol, a hatchet (also handy for smashing saloons), a shotgun or an elaborate trap baited with money-bags or liquor.

Nor are the man-crazed Leap Year ladies particularly fussy about the object of their chase. They're shown to be delighted with a hugely obese victim, a scruffy bum, a drunk under the bed, a foolish looking lout, or a burglar breaking into a bedroom.

Often the women matched the stereotype of the desperate spinster with no charms to attract a man, but even when the female huntress was attractive, she baited her trap with goodies like sacks of money.

The battle of the sexes raged on postcards through 1912, then faded away as the fad for collecting and sending cards dwindled. In their heyday, however, they were a socially acceptable way of ridiculing women who wanted to assume a role traditionally reserved for men.

Leap Year postcards are fun to collect. They're plentiful enough to assemble a collection of hundreds and not nearly as expensive as high-end cards like Halloween greetings. The next time you see an old postcard with a predatory woman jumping on a man from behind, ask yourself what the original purchaser was thinking. Was it really so ridiculous for a woman to take the initiative in proposing marriage?

THE QUEST FOR OLYMPIC GOLD – ON POSTCARDS

Paris tried to kill me.

Food poisoning would have been enough for one visit, but I was knocked over when a crowd surged forward in an elevator going down to the subway and tripped up by a vicious piece of metal sticking out of the ground near the Arc de Triomphe. It was a relief to get on a train for Rome until an electrical fire under our sleeping car provided a little more excitement.

But without bloody knees from my encounter with partially buried debris, I never would have sought sanctuary in that most American of refuges: MacDonald's. And guess what! They were giving away a free postcard in support of the French team going to the 1996 summer Olympics in Atlanta. The card I brought home was a unique addition to my small Olympics collection and one I was unlikely to see again anywhere else.

The modern Olympics came into being when an international com-

Jesse Owens

mittee was formed in 1894. The first summer games were held, very appropriately, in Athens in 1896 and have continued to the present with timeouts for two world wars.

It's possible to put together a stunning collection of postcards promoting the games, but many carry a high price tag. A quick check of eBay prices showed an asking price of $500 for a futuristic Italian design for the 1932 Los Angeles Olympics, $250 for a real photo of an athlete at the same event, and $100 to $300 for cards from the 1940s and '50s.

But no collector need be discouraged by upper-end prices and a scarcity of early cards. Every Olympics has been commemorated by postcards, both the summer games and the winter games that now alternate every two years.

One of the flashiest series was issued by the U.S. Postal Service for the 1996 games. They were postal cards with the stamp design on the front, but they could also be ordered as first-day-of-issue cards with the stamp matching the design, cancelled on the front.

If government-issued cards seem too commercial, there are official ones licensed by the United States Olympics Committee. Use of the distinctive five rings has to be authorized.

It's easy to find postage stamps issued for the games, but the trick is to find them used on postcards related to the places where they're held. Ones sent by travelers or visitors to the games are more desirable than those created by and for collectors.

The cities that host the Olympics invest a great deal in building new facilities. Postcards showing the arenas, stadiums, ski runs and other construction still in use after the event have a place in an Olympics collection, but my favorite post-Olympics card shows Jesse Owens, winner of four gold medals in 1936. Adolph Hitler hoped to prove the myth of Aryan superiority in the Berlin Olympics, banning Jewish and Romany (gypsy) athletes from his highly trained team, but an African-American was the most outstanding athlete of the games and the era.

National pride and love of spectacle make the Olympics far more important than just another athletic event. Enjoy them again and again on postcards.

COLLECTORS HOWL FOR COSTUMES ON VINTAGE HALLOWEEN POSTCARDS

My youngest granddaughter has a bumblebee costume for Halloween, but she won't do any trick-or-treating, at least not until she learns to walk. She's typical of a whole generation of children whose parents delight in dressing them in weird and colorful costumes for the spooky holiday.

Many Halloween traditions can be traced back to observances for the festival of Samhain, a sort of Celtic New Year, which marked the end of the light half of the year and the beginning of the dark. It was a night when spirits of the dead could cross back into this world, and some of them were nasty and frightening. The only protection against them was to wear a disguise that fooled the evil beings.

The huge influx of immigrants, particularly Irish refugees from the potato famine of the mid 19th century, brought with them traditions dating back to the Middle Ages, but Americans made the holiday their own in the early 20th century. Halloween postcards tell the story of celebrations that included ghosts, witches, black cats and leering jack-o'-lanterns, but the real fun came in dressing up. In the first decade of the 1900s, Halloween costumes were mostly worn by adults, and many parties were for grownups.

Real photo postcards show groups in costume, sometimes all alike or following a theme. But like all fads from blind-man's bluff to whist, these costume parties gradually grew out of favor, but the fun of Halloween lived on with children. Trick-or-treating didn't become a widespread way of celebrating Halloween until the 1930s, and manufactured costumes began appearing in stores in that decade.

Still, this was the time of the Great Depression, and homemade costumes were much more common. Old bed sheets were easy to turn into ghost costumes, and all a tramp needed was old clothing, a bundle on a stick and black shoe polish as makeup. An old black dress could be scaled down for a witch costume, and black construction paper made a satisfactory pointed hat.

Girls who were lucky enough to have a mother who sewed, and many did in the 1930s, could dress as Cinderella or a fairy godmother.

The Dennison Company even issued pamphlets giving directions for costumes using their crepe paper. (Not for wet weather or the snow that frequently made a Halloween appearance in the Midwest.) Whether children went for scary or pretty, homemade was the norm.

One church in our town has a Halloween event called "Trunk or Treat." Children dress in their costumes and go to open car trunks in the parking lot. Undoubtedly, it's a safe way for them to beg for candy, but it makes a person nostalgic for the scary fun of racing from house to house on a dark street, perhaps chased by older boys with mischief in mind. Our porch light will be on for trick-or-treating, and no doubt a parade of costumed children will arrive with pillowcases already bulging with candy. And hopefully, among the manufactured costumes, there will be some original creations like the bunch of grapes that one girl wore a few seasons ago.

All it took was purple balloons, a lot of air, and a good imagination. One thing is sure. There will be witches, ghosts, devils, vampires, skeletons, and even aliens on our doorstep.

Scary costumes are at the heart of Halloween fun today as they were on early postcards.

TEN-HUT! CELEBRATE VETERAN'S DAY WITH U.S. SOLDIERS ON VINTAGE POSTCARDS

At their best, vintage postcards tell a story. One of the most poignant is the fate of millions of veterans who served their country at the highest cost to themselves and their families.

As early as 1811, the government recognized the need for a place where veterans could find a home when age and infirmities made independent living difficult or impossible. It took until 1834 for the first facility to open, the United States Naval Home in the Philadelphia Naval Yard.

The first soldiers' home was established in 1851 in Washington, D.C. The Old Soldiers' Home, now known as the Armed Forces Retirement Home, was followed by the establishment of many state and

Interior Dining Hall, Soldiers Home, Leavenworth, Kansas.

If I'm such a
joke SOMEBODY ought
to be laughing

Camp Custer. Mich.

Eagle Lake.

Electric Station, National Soldiers Home. Togus, Me.

federal homes, including some that accepted widows and orphans. When the Veterans Administration was formed in 1930, this agency took over the administration of 15 of the 17 federal homes.

States and benevolent organizations such as the Grand Army of the Republic and United Confederate Veterans were involved in starting more homes, most taken over by the states. By 1933, 43 states managed 55 homes for elderly and disabled veterans.

Cities, too, became active in establishing hostels for veterans, some evolving into homes for disabled servicemen. Women activists helped establish charitable homes in Boston, Chicago and Milwaukee. During the Civil War, the U.S. Sanitary Commission operated 18 soldiers' homes, 11 lodges and one rest home in 15 states to meet the needs of discharged and disabled veterans.

In all, 75 "historic" homes were established in response to the huge number of Civil War veterans, many of which went on to accept World War I vets. Many of these were substantial structures built in the best late Victorian tradition, the kind of buildings that appeal to collectors when they appear on Golden Age (early 1900s) postcards.

Many communities were proud of their old soldiers' homes, but

6680. Exterior, Dining Hall, Soldiers' Home, Leavenworth, Kansas.

5663. Lake Jeanette and Band Stand, Soldiers' Home, Leavenworth, Kansas.

postcards showing them aren't nearly as plentiful as more commonly collected courthouses, churches, post offices and other public buildings. Views showing the quality of life in the homes are even harder to find.

The Soldiers' Home in Leavenworth, Kan., was fairly well documented on circa 1910 postcards, showing a large facility with multiple buildings, including a separate dining hall. It was situated on Lake Jeanette with rolling lawns and a bandstand. It's near Leavenworth National Cemetery and was originally the Western Branch of the National Home for Disabled Volunteer Soldiers. The medical facility was transferred to the Veterans Administration in 1930.

The site was originally part of a Delaware Indian Reservation. By 1886, there were 17 structures on the property. The first trolley line went through the town to connect Fort Leavenworth and the Soldiers' Home. Because the original black and white photographs were colored for postcards by people who may never have seen the facility, the veterans are all shown in dark blue, making them still look like an army. A plus on any postcard is the presence of the men.

Postcards featuring veterans are often found priced as low as $1 to as high as $25 depending on the subject matter. When they can be found, Old Soldiers' Homes are touching reminders of the price veterans paid for their country. They definitely belong in any history-based collection.

THANKSGIVING POSTCARDS BEAUTIFUL BUT SKETCHY ON FACTS

Thanksgiving postcards are easy to find, colorful, and reasonably priced, for the most part. Almost every publisher in the early 1900s issued greetings for the holiday, but do they tell anything about the Pilgrims they commemorate?

The history behind Thanksgiving is pretty well known. A small group landed on Plymouth Rock in December 1620 and hoped to found a colony with freedom to practice religion as they pleased.

They're not to be confused with the Puritans of Massachusetts Bay Colony and Salem witchcraft fame. In later years, there was some hostility between the two groups. The Pilgrims' first winter was hor-

❧ The Mayflower Compact ❧

❧ In the Name of God, Amen. We whose names are underwritten, the loyal subjects of our dread sovereign Lord, King James, by the grace of God, of Great Britain, France and Ireland King, Defender of the Faith, etc.,

Having undertaken, for the glory of God, and advancement of the Christian faith and honor of our King and Country, a voyage to plant the first colony in the northern parts of Virginia, do by these presents solemnly and mutually in the presence of God, and one of another, covenant and combine ourselves together into a civil body politic, for our better ordering and preservation and furtherance of the ends aforesaid; and by virtue hereof to enact, constitute and frame such just and equal laws, ordinances, acts, constitutions and offices, from time to time, as shall be thought most meet and convenient for the general good of the Colony: unto which we promise all due submission and obedience.

In witness whereof we have hereunder subscribed our names at Cape Cod the *11 of November, in the year of the reign of our sovereign Lord, King James of England, France and Ireland the eighteenth, and of Scotland the fifty-fourth. Ano. Dom. 1620.

John Carver	Edward Tilly	Degory Priest
William Bradford	John Tilly	Thomas Williams
Edward Winslow	Francis Cooke	Gilbert Winslow
William Brewster	Thomas Rogers	Edmond Margeson
Isaac Allerton	Thomas Tinker	Peter Brown
Myles Standish	John Rigdale	Richard Britteridge
John Alden	Edward Fuller	George Soule
Samuel Fuller	John Turner	Richard Clarke
Christopher Martin	Francis Eaton	Richard Gardiner
William Mullins	James Chilton	John Allerton
William White	John Crackston	Thomas English
Richard Warren	John Billington	Edward Doty
John Howland	Moses Fletcher	Edward Leister
Stephen Hopkins	John Goodman	*Old calendar

John Alden and Priscilla.

rible. Half of the 102 who landed died, including 10 of 17 male heads of households. But in spite of the hardships and death, they got lucky in one important way. Instead of meeting hostile natives, they were greeted by Samoset, an Abnaki who had picked up some English from fishing boat captains. (Remember, the Pilgrims were not the first to journey to the New World.) The initial contact with Native Americans led to help from Squanto, who had been to England and mastered their

Copyright 1905 by the Rotograph Co.

50796   Myles Standish House, built 1666, South Duxbury, Mass.

A. S. Burbank, Plymouth, Mass.

Has you one like this? Olireni

SARCOPHAGUS. COLES HILL. PLYMOUTH. MASS.

language. Most important of all, the Patuxets leader, Massasoit, initiated a peace treaty with the newcomers.

Thanks to the help of the Native Americans and a bountiful harvest in 1621, the Pilgrims' future looked better. They held a feast to give thanks to God for their deliverance. The Virginian colonists had held a similar harvest celebration, and it was common practice in many European communities. In fact, any group that survived a year in the New World had reason to be thankful.

The idea of a Thanksgiving Day spread throughout the colonies. Colonial governors issued annual proclamations, and President Washington declared a general day of thanksgiving in 1789. Sarah Josepha Hale, editor of *Godey's Lady's Book*, pressured presidents for 20 years to establish Thanksgiving as an annual holiday. In 1863, President Lincoln appointed the last Thursday in November as Thanksgiving Day. It was observed on this date until 1941, when President Franklin D. Roosevelt changed it to the fourth (but not final) Thursday in November.

Postcard makers liked to focus on one particular aspect of the holiday: a turkey for Thanksgiving dinner. It's very likely that wild turkeys were among the fowl hunted in 1621, but the birds tended to push the Pilgrims into the background on early 20th century postcards. When Pilgrims are pictured, they're shown in dark, plain costumes with bland expressions that reveal little of the personalities that dared the new world.

The history-minded collector won't find many Thanksgiving cards of interest, but Massachusetts remembered its founding fathers and commemorated them on postcards sold over the last hundred years.

They're not likely to be listed in a "Pilgrim" category in a show dealer's stock, but they're out there. Tracing the footsteps of people who lived nearly 400 years ago is a challenge, but it can add an extra dimension to the modern holiday devoted to turkey and football.

MADE IN THE U.S.A. – THANKSGIVING POSTCARDS

Sending, receiving and collecting postcards was a worldwide mania that began in the 1890s and continued until public tastes changed around 1914. The early 20th century was the "Golden Age." The superstars among publishers, firms like Tuck, Finkenrath and International Art, had one thing in common; their cards were manufactured in Germany, the world's print shop at that time. This doesn't mean that enterprising American printers weren't trying to capture the market. Two particularly prolific U.S. companies were Edw. H. Mitchell and the Detroit Publishing Co., both specializing in views.

Improbable as it seems, postcards that sold for as little as a penny were big business, but American printers were hard-pressed to compete with the Germans. The answer was a protective tariff. The Payne-Aldrich Act was enacted 1909, leveling the playing field by charging customs on imported postcards (based on weight, not the count).

The door was open for Americans to expand into the lucrative postcard market. Domestic firms could now aspire to dominate the market. Unfortunately it didn't work out quite that way. No bill gets through the U.S. Congress overnight, and wholesalers had plenty of time to stockpile German-made cards. In fact, they bought up so many that they became a glut on the market.

In 1912, the retail giant, Woolworth, became a serious player. They started selling postcards for 10 cents a dozen in their hundreds of stores. Profits shrunk, and so did demand.

Postcards didn't fade away overnight, but the craze for them dropped significantly as public tastes changed. Victorian and Art Nouveau slowly gave way to the crisper, livelier style now called Art Deco, and postcard buying dwindled.

Beginning in 1912, the public was introduced to an alternative to postcard greetings when the first folded cards with mailing envelopes came onto the market. Even though they sold for the princely sum of 5 cents each, they caught on with people who wanted something special in greetings. And face it, if friends sent a Christmas card discreetly mailed in an envelope, wouldn't it be a bit old-fashioned to return a postcard?

In spite of adverse conditions, some American printers still made a go of postcards. These latter-day U.S. publishers deserve more attention from collectors, particularly at a time when nothing in retail stores seems to have been made in this country.

Who were they? George C. Whitney of Worcester, Mass. is the best known. His company made valentines in the 19th century and postcard greetings in the 20th. The firm was liquidated in 1942, but not before making a great many cards, many picturing children. They have a distinctive logo with the company name, making them easy to identify.

A.M. Davis of Boston began making postcards in 1908, at first using his own art and verses. His greetings were printed on heavy stock and sometimes had a distinctive border around the edges. He was one of the early makers of greetings with envelopes, which made his business successful when other printers were going bankrupt.

The Gibson Art Co. was prolific into the 1920s and published Rose O'Neill's and Bernhardt Wall's charming art. P.F. Volland & Co. of Chicago, best known as the publisher of Raggedy Ann books, also issued a long series of unique and highly desirable cards. The Fairman Co. of Cincinnati published greetings and comics that featured the art of Dulk, Farini and Kemble. Gartner & Bender of Chicago had some winners with Kewpie types (unsigned) and kids like those of Charles Twelvetrees.

This is by no means a complete list. Some American publishers made a brief appearance then disappeared. Others, like Whitney, persevered to leave behind an impressive number of collectible cards.

Wish yourself a happy Thanksgiving by adding some American-made greetings to your collection. They're just as much fun as the imports of the Golden Age.

ARE POSTCARDS TRUE TO PILGRIMS?

Thanksgiving postcards are easy to find, colorful, and reasonably priced, for the most part. Almost every publisher in the early 1900s issued greetings for the holiday, but do they tell anything about the Pilgrims they commemorate?

The history behind Thanksgiving is pretty well known. A small group landed on Plymouth Rock in December 1620 and hoped to found a colony with freedom to practice religion as they pleased.

They're not to be confused with the Puritans of Massachusetts Bay Colony and Salem witchcraft fame. In later years, there was some hostility between the two groups. The Pilgrims' first winter was horrible. Half of the 102 who landed died, including 10 of 17 male heads of households. But in spite of the hardships and death, they got lucky in one important way. Instead of meeting hostile natives, they were greeted by Samoset, an Abnaki who had picked up some English from fishing boat captains. (Remember, the Pilgrims were not the fist to journey to the New World.) The initial contact with

Native Americans led to help from Squanto, who had been to England and mastered their language. Most important of all, the Patuxets leader, Massasoit, initiated a peace treaty with the newcomers.

Thanks to the help of the Native Americans and a bountiful harvest in 1621, the Pilgrims' future looked better. They held a feast to give thanks to God for their deliverance. The Virginian colonists had held a similar harvest celebration, and it was common practice in many European communities. In fact, any group that survived a year in the New World had reason to be thankful. The idea of a Thanksgiving Day spread throughout the colonies. Colonial governors issued annual proclamations, and President Washington declared a general day of thanksgiving in 1789.

Sarah Josepha Hale, editor of *Godey's Lady's Book*, pressured presidents for 20 years to establish Thanksgiving as an annual holiday. In 1863, President Lincoln appointed the last Thursday in November as Thanksgiving Day. It was observed on this date until 1941, when President Franklin D. Roosevelt changed it to the fourth (but not final) Thursday in November.

Postcard makers liked to focus on one particular aspect of the holiday: a turkey for Thanksgiving dinner. It's very likely that wild turkeys were among the fowl hunted in 1621, but the birds tended to push the Pilgrims into the background on early 20th century postcards. When Pilgrims are pictured, they're shown in dark, plain costumes with bland expressions that reveal little of the personalities that dared the new world. The history-minded collector won't find many Thanksgiving cards of interest, but Massachusetts remembered its founding fathers and commemorated them on postcards sold over the last hundred years.

They're not likely to be listed in a "Pilgrim" category in a show dealer's stock, but they're out there. Tracing the footsteps of people who lived nearly 400 years ago is a challenge, but it can add an extra dimension to the modern holiday devoted to turkey and football.

THE MAN WHO PUT GLAMOUR INTO THANKSGIVING

When it comes to postcards, Thanksgiving is not the most exciting holiday. Turkeys, alive or on a platter, can hardly compete with a Halloween witch or a jolly old Santa. As for the pilgrims who are associated with the original Thanksgiving, most of them could have benefited from the services of America's favorite makeover show, "What Not to Wear."

The most noteworthy exception is the work of Samuel L. Schmucker. No doubt collectors have always been attracted to the lovely women published by the Detroit Publishing Company and John Winsch, but it wasn't until the publication of an important book that the artist became widely recognized within the hobby.

Picture Postcards in the United States 1893-1918 by George and Dorothy Miller came out in 1976 bringing factual information about Schmucker and his publishers to the attention of postcard enthusiasts. The authors researched a great many sources, the most important of which were the Library of Congress and the United States Copyright Office. (The book was reprinted in 1982 under the name Dorothy B. Ryan.)

Unlike much noteworthy postcard art, Schmucker's was unsigned, the only exception being the occasional use of his initials, S.L.S. After his work was illustrated and discussed in the Miller book, collectors could put a name to cards that were already prized for their quality. Excitement escalated with the discovery of some original art, making Schmucker one of the most popular American postcard artists. Samuel L. Schmucker was born in Reading, Pa., in 1879 and began his training at the Pennsylvania Academy of Fine Arts. Like artists throughout the ages, he had to face the problem of how to make a living, so he studied commercial art at the Howard Pyle Institute.

Postcards are his best-remembered art, although he put his hand to other types of illustrating from fashion prints to candy boxes. Unfortunately he died in 1921 at the age of 42. The hallmark of a really good artist is a unique style. Once a collector becomes familiar with a few examples of Schmucker's work, it's not hard to spot others. Color is the first clue.

Even after nearly a hundred years, they're still warm and vibrant with wonderful shadowing and brushwork. He made pink cheeks glow and never stinted on the use of a broad palette of colors. Unlike lesser artists, his background designs are highly detailed and add to the overall effect. He used his wife Katherine as a model but varied hair colors and costumes to avoid sameness. The fineness of his work helps to explain why people at the time would pay more for a Winsch postcard, sometimes as much as five cents when poorer quality cards were available for a penny.

Needless to say, a collection of Schmucker postcards involves a serious investment. Thanksgiving ladies are modestly priced compared to Halloween subjects, but expect to pay $50 or more for a card in excellent condition. Above all, study before you buy. There's much information online and in books to guide the collector who's attracted to this fine American artist.

TOYS ENHANCE VINTAGE CHRISTMAS POSTCARDS

Sometimes it's the little details that make a postcard stand out from similar ones. This is certainly true of Christmas cards that show the toys children might expect from Santa Claus in the early 1900s. The toys spilling out of Santa's bag tell a story all their own and add to the charm of the artwork.

Postcards and toys have one big thing in common: The earliest and best ones were made in Germany. In fact, the toy industry began long before the postcard craze of the early 1900s. As early as the 14th century wood carvers in the southern part of the country were turning out animal figures to be sold by peddlers.

Early toys were manufactured to teach children how to become adults. In the 18th century that meant tin armies for boys and miniature kitchens for girls, but toys were mostly given to the children of the wealthy. It wasn't until the mid 19th century that middle class children might own a manufactured plaything. Cheap composition doll heads and lithographed paper on play sets put toys within the price range of people of more modest means.

By the late 1800s, a more affluent middle class meant that children were given time to play. While the offspring of the poor still labored on farms, mines and factories or cared for younger siblings, the more fortunate might play with building blocks, miniature tools, dolls, or scaled down household implements.

The first decade of the 20th century was the Golden Age of postcards, but it also saw a great demand for both imported and American-made playthings. As more children were freed from the work force, the market for toys grew. A middle class home might have board games, card games, toy trains and other vehicles, crafts, and toys that demonstrated scientific principles. There was a definite gender division, with girls expected to like baby dolls best.

In 1906 a new craze hit the toy market just in time to be shown on postcards: the Teddy Bear. It was a cuddly stuffed toy that a child could cherish for a feeling of security. Based on the story that Teddy Roosevelt spared the life of a baby bear while hunting, the new toy became an instant hit. A Teddy Bear on a postcard can date it to post-1906.

Toys can be found on many Santa postcards as well as those that show angels delivering gifts.

Toys under a Christmas tree aren't quite as common, but these scenes can include larger toys like rocking horses that wouldn't fit well in Santa's bag. Some especially charming postcards picture children playing with their Christmas toys.

Santa is well loved by collectors, but when he has a bag overflowing with the toys children played with in the early 1900s, his popularity should soar.

GNOMES FOR CHRISTMAS FUN

Gnomes have grown. They began as tiny creatures in legends that go back a thousand years in Europe. Supposedly they lived a subterranean lifestyle and were so tiny they could hide behind a toadstool.

Unlike some mythical beings that are dangerous and evil, gnomes are good-hearted and helpful. They reputedly help farmers and tend gardens by night, acts of kindness that led to the first garden gnomes, terracotta figures produced in Germany in the mid-1800s. Only one survived from the original lot brought to Great Britain in 1847. Supposedly it's insured for a million pounds now. In their modern incarnation, they're sturdy little dwarves who promote a travel service on TV.

Unlike the elves who help Santa, gnomes came onto the Christmas scene by helping the goats that delivered sleighs full of gifts in 16th-century Sweden. Belief in them faded until the 19th century when their legends resurfaced, promoted in stories like those collected by the Brothers Grimm.

Gnomes never came to mind when I bid on and won an auction lot of miniature Swedish postcards. I've always been fascinated by tiny cards that have passed through the mail, and the estimate of $12 for 32 Christmas cards was too good to pass up. As hoped, some had gone through the mail with stamps in tact between the 1930s and 1970s, and one even had a delightful Swedish Christmas seal. The real bonus was in the gnomes, 10 different ones, all with the distinctive red-peaked hat. One was a very Art Deco girl gnome, and one was a child gnome. The rest were white-bearded men with wooden shoes doing things to help people, including tending a horse.

Best of all, three were signed by Erik Forsman (1916-1976), the Swedish book illustrator who did much to revive the lore of gnomes. His postcards were among the newer ones in the auction lot, used in the '70s. A skilled artist, he gave gnomes distinct personalities and charming expressions, making his work well worth collecting.

Checking on eBay, I also found his art on a full-size postcard with a rooster making a speech to hens and chicks, showing that his range went beyond mythical gnomes.

Without artists to make gnomes come alive, it seems unlikely that any would have reached the big-time, namely the TV gig and popularity as garden statues. Forsman was one of the best, but not the first.

Postcard collectors are more familiar with Jenny Nystrom, an earlier Swedish artist who popularized the mythical creatures. A collection of postcard gnomes is well within the reach of most collectors. Their red hats, probably adapted from those worn by Mediterranean fisherman because they couldn't be seen in the dark, are the one sure way to identify them.

Although gnomes seem devoted to good works now, older versions had a gnarled old man living underground and guarding buried treasure. At one time this image was so familiar that Swiss bankers were called the Gnomes of Zurich.

Since many appear on foreign-made postcards, it's helpful to know that they're called Tomten in Sweden, Kaukis in Germany, and Barbegazi in France and Switzerland where they are pictured with big feet.

As much as collectors love the old-time Christmas postcards of the early 1900s, there's a great deal of pleasure to be had from later ones. European greetings from the 1930s on are still plentiful at give-away prices and may well become highly sought-after collectibles in the future.

HALLOWEEN POSTCARDS

From the editors of Antique Trader

Halloween postcards seem to be a very stable commodity in the postcard world. For the last 30 years, I have seen the price grow from a couple of dollars a card to $1,500 for some. While the prices for individual cards may fluctuate from time to time, there has never been a drastic drop, a true blue chip of the industry. Why might this be?

The factors that seem to have played a major role in this sector of postcards being collected is it seems to be a holiday that all adults relate to having had it play some part in their lives as children. The attraction to the holiday is the fun of costumes, candy and being allowed to run free and be a bit naughty without fear of punishment. It is the one time of the year that children are free to run wildly through neighborhoods after dark. Just pure excitement abounds everywhere from school parties to parades to crazy fun with friends.

The postcards of Halloween for the most part are extremely colorful and well done. The history portrayed on the cards relate to the past importance of the time as being a major step in courtship which would lead to a successful marriage, maybe as soon as Spring. Many of the traditions relate to women trying to determine who their true love may be. One Halloween card features a couple hanging as ornaments on a Christmas tree with the verse, "Your face I've seen on Halloween, Will you be my little Queen?" this reaffirms the importance of Halloween as a source of finding a spouse. This card recently sold for $175 in the Lyn Knight Auction.

Because the postcards were produced for the American market, the number is more limited than holidays that were celebrated around the world. By collectors' counts the total number of images produced for Halloween, excluding any real photo postcards is about 3500 images. It is only recently that the European collectors have become extremely excited over the Halloween postcards and are becoming a major buying force in this topic on eBay.

Of all the Halloween postcards collected, the publisher John O. Winsch of Stapleton, New York, is the publisher of choice when buying high quality, steadily increasing values and great design. The Winsch postcards designed by Samuel L Schmucker have always been on the list of must haves. The main company of John Winsch was only in business a short time. It is generally known that Winsch started business in 1910, really reached its peak in 1911 and then stop producing cards in 1915. However, a collector has recently pointed out to me he has had Winsch cards with copyright dates into the 20s but not of the standards of the early cards.

Winsch like many publishers of their time would hire artists to design graphic art for them and would become owners of this art. To save added costs, publishers would combine parts of images from one artists work with that of another to create a new design for a postcard. While it was frustrating to the artist to see his work be cut and pasted with others of perhaps lesser quality, it was a standard practice.

One of the funniest examples of that to me is the Frexias Halloween card of the child taking a lid off a pumpkin, which was later used as a Valentine by replacing the base of the pumpkin with a heart. However, they neglected to remove the pumpkin lid from the child's hand.

Many of the Winsch postcards illustrated here have pieces of Schmucker's work used as background with children that have been designed by a different artist. Look carefully at the images. In one case the top postcard has been divided in two with the top half of the image being a background on one card and the bottom half of the image as a background on a different postcard.

These types of designs confuse beginning collectors. I am frequently asked, "Is this a Schmucker?" And the answer has to be, well, yes and no. He did the background work.

Enjoy the images illustrated here but examine them to see the cross over from one card to another.

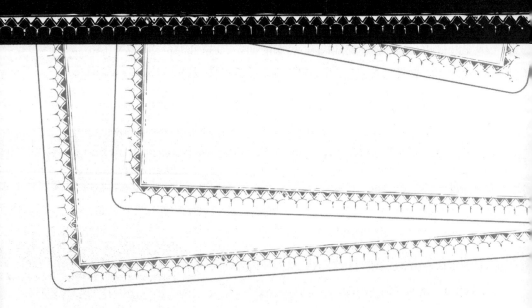

CHAPTER 4

PLACES ON POSTCARDS

Menephtah avec les attributes d' Osiride fait des offres à Ammone et à Knoum.
Menephtah with the attributs of Osiride makes offres to Ammone and to Knoum.

ANCIENT EGYPT: WHERE TOURISTS GO, VINTAGE POSTCARDS FOLLOW

What do Alexander the Great, Caesar and Napoleon have in common — aside from being ruthless conquerors? If their time in Egypt comes to mind, you're 100 percent correct.

Alexander lingered there to explore the mysteries of the ancient religion. Caesar spent time bonding with the last Pharaoh, Cleopatra. And Napoleon brought an army, hoping to take the country away from the Ottoman Empire. None of these famous military men can be called tourists, but their interest reflects the awe and fascination people of all ages have had for Egypt.

Nobody built as many elaborate tombs as the ancient Egyptians. From the massive pyramids made for Pharaohs to the secret laby-

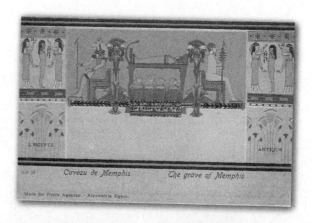

Caveau de Memphis   The grave of Memphis

Made for Pierre Agopian - Alexandria Egypt.

The high priest and his assistants performing the ceremony of "Opening the Mouth" on the mummy of Hunefer at the door of the tomb. Anubis embraces the mummy and Nasha, the wife of Hunefer, and his daughter kneel before it weeping.

rinths in the Valley of the Kings, thousands of years of history are wonderfully preserved. These wonders have been a magnet for travelers from Roman times to the present.

Tourists must have souvenirs. Napoleon brought a host of scholars and artists along with his army and managed to snag the Rosetta stone. His people were only the vanguard of an army of archeologists and looters who helped themselves to tons of priceless artifacts now housed in museums worldwide. (The Egyptians would like them back, of course.)

Between Napoleon's aborted attempt to conquer Egypt and Howard Carter's discovery of King Tut's tomb in 1924, the country be-

came the ultimate traveler's destination. Fortunately, not every tourist could afford to ship a mummy or a priceless artifact home. For those with greater scruples or less cash, postcards hit the racks in the early 1900s.

Like every other country, Egypt sold a lot of cards showing local attractions. The pyramids, the Sphinx and temple ruins are common scenic cards. Native types are less common, but not rare. The ultimate fascination for visitors is the ancient art. No high-status tomb was complete without extensive wall paintings with religious significance. The story of ancient Egypt is preserved in the burial places, thanks in great part to the dry climate.

The most beautiful postcards to come out of Egypt are artist-drawn reproductions of the tomb art. Three series from the early 1900s especially stand out for their subtle but lovely coloring and attention to detail. The first was published by J.D. Auria in Cairo. There are at least 18 cards in the series, all printed with undivided backs that have a red border and both French and Egyptian writing on the address side. Some, but not all, have a caption in English, as well as French.

De Giogio of Cairo published several lettered series with at least six postcards in each. The backs are the same as Auria's, suggesting that they were printed by one firm and sold to individual publishers. A third series, also using the same back, was made for Pierre Agopian of Alexandria. The highest-numbered card in my collection is No. 25, but there could be others. None of the cards I've seen have been mailed, suggesting that travelers bought them as keepsakes.

To round out a collection of Egyptian art cards, it's necessary to look for those made by The British Museum. They were issued in series designated by letters and numbers. B 52 is the highest numeral in my collection, while the mummy series are all C's. These, too, have undivided backs, but unlike the Egyptian issues, they were printed on heavy card stock. The color is good, but not as outstanding as on the Egyptian-made postcards.

This is only a sampling of how widespread the production of Egyptian souvenir postcards was during the 20th century. Sometimes there was artistic license, in that the artists didn't produce exact copies of tomb art, but their work adds beauty and interest to any collection.

JAMESTOWN REVISITED

Sometimes postcards reveal attitudes that the original makers didn't intend. Consider this postcard issued for the Jamestown Exposition in 1907 that celebrated the 300th anniversary of the settlement. The entire message area on the back has a long explanation of the portrait on the front.

It reads, in part: "POCAHONTAS. An idealized portrait made at the time she was in England. Virginia cannot too much honor the memory of this lovely young woman, since to her more than once Virginia owed its existence. And so long as history records deeds dared and hardships endured by the first settlers at Jamestown, so long will Pocahontas be remembered as the guardian angel of the colony."

In the 100 years since this was written, archaeologists have been hard at work uncovering evidence of the true story of Jamestown, and historians have re-evaluated popular legends. Whether or not Pocahontas ever threw herself on John Smith to save his life, it's far more likely that her father, King Powhatan, acted from political motives, perhaps hoping to avoid open conflict with the strange people intruding on his territory.

One myth that has been undercut is that the "gentlemen" settlers wouldn't work. In fact, recent digs have revealed a diversified settlement with cultural remains that suggest the colony was involved in a variety of occupations. The biggest revelation is the way the English lifestyle impacted negatively on the environment enjoyed by Native Americans. Add to this the horrible death toll from European diseases, especially smallpox, and the story of Jamestown is very different from the one told a hundred years ago.

Look again at the portrait that symbolized the Jamestown Expo in 1907. It shows a very light-skinned woman with the tiny rosebud mouth that was considered especially beautiful at the time. Although the caption says that this is an "idealized" portrait, it doesn't admit that no one would mistake this person for a Native American. The artist thought he was honoring Pocahontas by giving her the plump, pale body admired in English gentlewomen at the time. In fact, reproducing this portrait as a symbol of the exposition did a great disservice to the real "little snow flower of Powhatan" as she's also described on the postcard.

Regardless of the attempt to make Pocahontas look like a pampered English gentlewoman, postcard makers issued some very worthwhile cards. The Jamestown Amusement and Vending Co. of Norfolk, Va., which published the Pocahontas card, was responsible for a set of 195 cards and an official catalog of the event, but this was only one of more than 50 firms that issued cards for the expo. Anyone interested in this event or other American expos would do well to locate a copy of American Exposition Postcards, 1870-1920, by Frederic and Mary Megson.

Although Jamestown A. & V.'s cards aren't the scarcest cards for this expo, they are particularly entertaining, thanks to the sometimes lengthy text on the backs. Card No. 15, Landing of the Maidens at Jamestown, provides this insight:

"In 1619 ninety young women of unexceptional character, who had volunteered for the purpose, arrived at Jamestown from England. Singular features of the arrangement were that the husband was to pay the cost of their outfit and passage in tobacco, 120 pounds, amounting to about $80, and a proclamation of the Governor that young women who betrothed themselves to more than one lover at a time would be severely punished."

So not only was Jamestown the first settlement, it was the first instance of mail-order brides, worth at that time their weight in tobacco.

STREET SCENE POSTCARDS ILLUSTRATE URBAN DEVELOPMENT

Collectors love postcards picturing the small towns and villages of the early 20th century, especially real photographs. Many of them existed to serve the needs of a predominantly rural population, but the last hundred years have brought a dramatic shift to a largely urban society. Approximately 80 percent of Americans now live in big towns and cities.

Each big city has a dynamic all its own. Imagine taking a mystery trip to some of the country's largest urban areas. How many could you

recognize without knowing where you were? Most likely you would recognize New York City, Philadelphia, Chicago, Denver, Phoenix, Los Angeles and a host of other mega cities.

Big cities started as trading posts, forts or villages, and each one has a unique history. In the late 19th and early 20th centuries hustle and bustle was a sign of progress, and postcard makers were quick

to publish a huge number of crowded street scenes. These cards are a historical treasure trove for any collector interested in the growth of the nation.

The best city street scenes show people, transportation, and "modern" innovations such as light poles, power lines, and streetcar tracks.

Sometimes "unsightly" features like networks of lines were removed in the manufacturing process to beautify the view, but the best cards show them.

The role of the street in people's lives is demonstrated again and again on big city postcards. Merchants set up shop on the streets, and people shopped, walked, and socialized outside in far greater numbers than is typical in most large cities today, with the exception of New York City and tourist areas.

Parades were a much bigger deal a hundred years ago when entertainment was more limited. Everything from a circus to a convention was a cause for a procession, and many were captured on postcards.

Public transportation in 1910 was easier to use than it is now. A streetcar line was the hallmark of a progressive city, and even relatively small towns might be linked by an interurban.

Sometimes horse-drawn conveyances, early motor vehicles, and pedestrians all vied for space on a city street. Postcards captured the dawn of the traffic jam, one urban problem that is still with us.

Night scenes are relatively scarce, but cities were proud of their first electric lights. They were another sign of progress and well worth a collector's time to find them.

Buildings in business districts were almost always crowded together, so signs had to be visible from a distance. The art of signs would make an interesting study, and almost every early street scene has a number of them. I've never seen one, but a card showing how sign painters worked on two story or even taller building walls would be a gem.

The treasure is in the details. In some cities the American flag flew from the rooftops of commercial buildings, not just government structures. A big water tank on a roof is a reminder that the threat of fire was very real, and a fire escape adds additional interest to a postcard. Colorful awnings hanging over the sidewalks were used before air conditioning when the streets could literally sizzle from the heat and clothing was anything but cool.

Keen-eyed collectors who like to spot early automobiles, streetcars, and clothing will find gold on 1910 era street scenes. It's rather amazing how carefully color was applied in the days before color photography, and another plus is a clear postmark dating the use of the card.

Big city street scenes are most likely to appeal to people who live in them, but there's something for everyone in these marvelous records of urban life a hundred years ago.

MESSAGES ON HUMANITARIAN POSTCARDS STILL RING TRUE

The terrible 2010 earthquake in Haiti horrified the world, and calls for relief funds were answered worldwide, proving that people are inherently generous and caring when given the opportunity.

The response was fueled by the truly amazing communications of the 21st century, especially computers and televisions that deliver immediate images of the disaster.

It wasn't always so. A hundred years ago even the best reporters had to telegraph their stories, and the public had to wait for the presses to roll. Fund raising for any cause was a slow process, but the lowly post-

Free Coal-Slum Work

Australian Aborigines' Mission.
Miss Baker, Secretary, - - La Perouse, N.S.W.

card played an important part.

Church groups often took the lead in providing food, medical care and educational opportunities in parts of the world where it was most needed. The fact that missionaries were motivated by a desire to spread their faith in no way diminishes the good they did.

Distributing food and medical care was expensive, so fund raising

DISTRIBUTION OF RICE AT THE DISPENSARY.

was an important part of any effort.

Pioneer aide workers certainly understood that one picture is worth a thousand words, and postcards supported fund raising efforts as effectively as any other medium available in the early 20th century.

They fall into three categories: scenes of humanitarian activities to stimulate donations, thanks for funds received and, less commonly, postcards sold to raise money for causes.

The Salvation Army was especially active with the poor, and that included working in this country's worst slums. A whole series of postcard scenes that included the work of "doughnut girls" in Europe during World War I were issued with requests for contributions printed on the back.

There's no doubt that church members in this country were charmed by scenes of little orphans in far-flung places like China, but some charitable groups used whatever postcards were available to send out requests for help. A good example of this is a scene of a Hawaiian luau with this message on the back:

"Dear Friend, Hawaii out here in the middle of the Pacific has already pledged its share of The American Legion Endowment Fund for Disabled men and the orphans of Veterans of the World War (I). The home folks should not do less 'For those who gave the most' in the Campaign now under way in the States."

People who donate once are likely to do so again, so some form of thank-you was important. One example of a postcard expressing thanks had a printed message and signature on the back of a picture of orphans at a Franciscan mission in China. Again, mailing postcards was often the cheapest possible way to spread a message and highlight humanitarian needs. Governments have the resources to respond to a disaster quicker than any private agency, as shown by the U.S. military presence in Haiti.

But what many people may not know is that one of our least popular presidents was also a great humanitarian. Before he was president, Herbert Hoover organized massive relief efforts for war torn Europe after World War I. He was Secretary of Commerce in 1927 when flooding of the lower Mississippi River left 1,500,000 people homeless and destroyed 2 million acres of cropland. He organized relief operations for the stricken area, and the story of his disaster responses is told in his library at West Branch, Iowa.

A postcard is just a little piece of paper, but many were used to rally help for disasters or fight the ravages of poverty. We'll never know how many people said "I can help" based on what they saw or read on a postcard, but there's no doubt that they played a part in the history of relief work.

POSTCARDS TELL OF DISASTER IN TEXAS CITY

Images from disasters and other major events are sent around the world so quickly today that it's easy to forget the limitations of news coverage before the information highway was built. In 1947, for example, Texas City, Texas, was virtually destroyed by the worst industrial accident in American history. Scenes of this horrendous catastrophe could be seen in grainy newspaper photos, in movie theater newsreels, in magazine coverage and on postcards.

Yes, postcards. Photographers the world over have been drawn to disaster since the camera became a portable tool, and in the first half of the 20th century, they sometimes marketed their work on postcards. The impact of this really hit home when Dorothy Dedlow of Florida recently donated seven real photos of the Texas City disaster to my semi-annual charity sale for hunger relief.

The Texas port city was devastated by fertilizer, foreshadowing the deliberate use of ammonium nitrate as an ingredient in the 1995 Oklahoma City bombing. On April 16, 1947, the SS Grandcamp, a former Liberty ship from WWII, was assigned to help in the rebuilding of Europe under French registry. Paper bags of the chemical fertilizer were packed in the hold, a common cargo at the time, along with small arms, ammunition, machinery and sisal. Longshoremen later reported that the bags seemed warm to the touch.

Shortly after eight in the morning, a fire was spotted in the engine room of the Grandcamp. It quickly spread to the hold, and steam was piped in as a means of saving cargo. Instead the temperature soared to the explosive temperature of 850 degrees Fahrenheit. The ship detonated in front of a crowd that had lined the shoreline to watch the firefighting effort.

The results were unimaginable. A mushroom cloud soared 2,000 feet and knocked two small planes from the air. The blast was heard 150 miles away and triggered the explosion of a second ship, the High Flyer, also loaded with ammonium nitrate. A tidal wave surged over 100 miles of shoreline, leveling 1,000 buildings on land and sinking virtually every ship in the harbor. More than 6,300 tons of steel from the ship blasted into the air at supersonic speed. Oil and chemical storage tanks burned, several plants including Monsanto and Union Carbide were destroyed, and more than 500 homes were lost.

The human toll included all of Texas City's volunteer firefighters and an official death toll of 581, although the count might have been considerably higher. Thousands suffered injuries. (The health risks of inhaling the fumes weren't considered.) Fires were still burning a week later in spite of the efforts of 200 firefighters who came from as far away as Los Angeles.

The disaster also resulted in the first class action lawsuit against the United States government. The Supreme Court later overturned a lower court's decision for the plaintiffs, but congress provided some compensation.

Many disaster postcards were printed and sold locally, but the Texas

City catastrophe must have held nationwide interest. The leading maker of real photo postcards in the United States, the L.L. Cook Co. of Milwaukee, printed the photographs. Each card is numbered. In this group they range from M527 to M697, although this doesn't necessarily mean that more than 150 different cards were made.

The cards not shown here include a large parking lot with the cars covered in ash, a high spray of water over a dock, the skeletal remains of a buildings with many workers below it, and a scene of workers searching a broad area for bodies.

Both the scale of the damage and the legal ramifications give these cards great historical value. CNN is faster in news coverage, but postcards of devastation that happened more than 60 years ago still evoke sympathy for the people of Texas City.

HAWAIIAN POSTCARDS SAY "ALOHA"

From the editors of Antique Trader

Hawaii became a unique tourist attraction early in the 20th century just as postcards were becoming firmly established as a means of colorful promotion and communication.

Early 1900s Hawaiian postcards typically might present views of natives gathering sugar cane or pineapples. Other views might depict residences of the former royal family.

A paradise in the middle of the Pacific Ocean, Hawaii was comprised of eight islands of the main group when it was governed entirely by royalty. When Hawaii's King Kalauaua died in 1891, his sister Queen Liliuokalani ascended to the throne. However as the region became more and more attractive as a trade base and possible military site, it became a prize territory.

Hawaii was proclaimed a republic briefly in 1894, but was finally annexed by the United States in 1898 by a joint resolution of Congress.

During the early 1900s the Hawaiian Islands were considered a first class or "organized" territory, which allowed a local legislature. Citizens who could speak, read, and write the English or Hawaiian language were granted voting rights. The United States saw the location of Hawaii as a prime site for military and naval operations throughout the first half of the 20th century. Those in the military became tourists, as did members of their families.

By the 1930s the economic control began to shift in part from wealthy landowners to organized labor and tourist interests. Historically sugar cane and pineapples had been major industries for the islands, and gradually they were overtaken by tourism.

In 1935 a major postcard producer, Curteich and Company of Chicago, issued views proclaiming Hawaii as "the world's enchanted island playground." Other Curteich postcards assured, "you find enchanted mountains and bewitching beaches, music and beauty everywhere." Postcard scenes include the National Park, Rainbow Falls, the Valley Island of Maui, and the Garden Island of Kauai. Also included were the scenic wonders of Nuuanu Pali, and the Mormon Temple at Lai.

"Perhaps you will be honored by a luau (native feast), and there you'll see the real Hawaiian hula," noted on Curt Teich souvenir folder. "The Hawaiians say if you visit the Islands once you'll always want to return. There is magic in coral reefs and slanting palms."

Of course tranquil Hawaii exploded into World War II with the attack on Pearl Harbor by Japanese forces in December of 1941. Hawaii continued to play a key role as a military base of operations throughout the decade of the 1940s.

During the 1940s, a number of postcards were published and marketed by the Royal Hawaiian Distributing Company in Honolulu. Such postcards offered colorful views of surfboard riding and canoeing at famed Waikiki Beach and swimming at Diamond Head. Postcards billed swimming as an activity available "year round, day or night, to enhance this land of enchantment."

Royal Hawaiian postcards of the 1940s often featured hula troupes, net fishing, the Royal Hawaiian hotel, native families in grass shacks, and the palace of the royal family. During the 1940s a number of black and white real photo postcards were made available to men and women in the military service to illustrate the islands for the folks back home.

HENRY RINN CAPTURES EARLY BALTIMORE'S TRIALS AND TRIUMPHS ON VINTAGE POSTCARDS

Charles Bush

If you had lived in Baltimore at the turn of the 20th century, chances are that you would have encountered Henry Rinn Jr. energetically roving the streets with his ever-present tripod and camera. Rinn regularly crisscrossed the city, capturing glimpses of life in Baltimore during the early 1900s. Then, retiring to his bedroom that functioned as a makeshift darkroom, Rinn would develop his images and transform them into much sought-after picture postcards.

Rinn began producing his first series of black-and-white picture postcards in 1898. One of these early Private Mailing Cards features a picture of the Johns Hopkins Hospital; it is No. 9 in a series of 160 cards. In the lower right corner of the picture are the words, "Henry Rinn, Jr. Publisher."

Sometime around 1900, Rinn moved his photographic operations to 423 Courtland St. in Baltimore. Unfortunately, Rinn's studio and all his photographic equipment and master files were lost in the Great Baltimore Fire of February 1904, the conflagration that reduced the majority of the city's downtown business district to rubble in a little over 24 hours.

Undaunted by his misfortune, Rinn grabbed a camera that he had at his home and began documenting the aftermath of the fire. Rinn sent these photographs to the E. C. Kropp Co. in Milwaukee, Wis., where they were made into a series of 13 black-and-white picture postcards. Rinn was soon back in business, publishing a series of five unnumbered black-and-white postcards.

By late 1907, the refurbishment of downtown Baltimore had been completed, thanks to a Herculean effort of the community. In typical Baltimore fashion, the city fathers decided to celebrate with a party, so Oct. 13-19 was designated as Home Coming Week. The event was publicized with many souvenir postcards, including a series of seven picture and illustrated postcards produced by Henry Rinn Jr.

Around this same time, Rinn began to send his photographic prints to Germany, where, using advanced technology, the prints were processed into full-color postcards. Between 1904 and 1915, Rinn published more than 250 color picture postcards of Baltimore landmarks.

Unique within Rinn's color postcard series is a subset of 12 cards that were published under the name Baltimore Art Publishing Co. It remains a mystery as to why just these 12 cards were published by the Baltimore Art Publishing Co.

Among collectors, the most popular of the postcards published by Henry Rinn Jr. remain his fancy-border cards. These cards were published in two series. The first series consisted of 13 cards featuring various views of Baltimore surrounded by natural borders. One of the cards in the first fancy-border series shows an interior view of the Baltimore Fish Market, enclosed within a border of lobsters. Additional cards in the first series include a view of Baltimore Harbor surrounded by a border of shrimp, the entrance to Druid Hill Park inside a pine-cone and Mount Vernon Place within an ivy leaf.

The second series of the fancy-border cards contained six cards. Each card shows a different nautical subject pictured within an oyster shell. For example, the sixth card in the series features the paddleboat Emma A. Ford.

Most of the postcards published by Henry Rinn Jr. are still available and can be obtained for reasonable prices. Cards from the black-and-white series and the color series run from $3 to $10 each. The Baltimore Fire cards go for somewhat more, as do the Home Coming Week cards. The most expensive and the most difficult to acquire of the Rinn cards are the fancy-border cards, which sell for anywhere from $10 to $50, depending on condition.

For postcard collectors with an interest in Baltimore, obtaining the postcards published by Henry Rinn Jr. is a must and is worth the time and the effort it will take to track them down.

POSTCARDS TELL ST. CLOUD, MINN., HISTORY

Karen Knapstein

Author Harold Zosel, a 48-year resident of St. Cloud and an active member of the Stearns History Museum, shares his personal historic photograph and postcard collection in "St. Cloud," a recent addition to the Postcard History Series from Arcadia Publishing, a leading publisher of local and regional history in the United States.

The contents of "St. Cloud," which includes more than 200 vintage photographs and postcards along with detailed accompanying captions, are arranged into three categories: Industry and Transportation, Main Street and Public Buildings, and People and Occasions.

St. Cloud was incorporated in 1856 when three existing towns merged into one. The majority of the pages are dedicated to Main Street and Public Buildings, but the other two chapters also deliver plenty of imagery and information to satisfy the local history buff.

Conventional history books tell a story and are illustrated with occasional relevant images with captions to tell where they fit in. A wonderful thing about "St. Cloud," and the rest of the Postcard History Series for that matter, is that the pictures and postcards bring history to life, and the photo captions clarify any ambiguity.

Zosel's goal for "St. Cloud" is to bring back fond memories and inspire colorful stories by long-time residents, and will give the newcomers and visitors a better background in how St. Cloud evolved. Zosel also hopes "that people will discover that there is so much on vintage postcards that is not anywhere else."

Once again, the Postcard History Series nicely illustrates American history, making it a relevant accompaniment for traditional history books, as well as a worthy addition to any deltiologist's library.

'SEATTLE' USES POSTCARDS TO CHART CITY'S HISTORY AND CURIOSITIES

Karen Knapstein

The latest addition to Arcadia Publishing's Postcard History Series is Seattle, by Mark Sundquist. Filled with images of historic postcards selected from the author's collection and the Pacific Northwest Postcard Club collection, Seattle offers views into the "queen city" from well over a century ago through its transformation into a booming metropolis.

The chronologically organized chapters in Seattle include "Seattle's Native American Heritage," followed by "Early Years," "The Making of a World-Class City," "Roaring Teens and Twenties," "Depression and War," "Postwar Prosperity," and finally, "Seattle and a Brief History of Postcards."

With an advantageous location for maritime commerce, the discovery of coal and gold, and an unrivaled entrepreneurial spirit, Seattle had all it needed to make a rapid transformation from a rough frontier village into a modern city.

Author Mark Sundquist is a third generation Seattle resident and a longtime member of the Pacific Northwest Postcard Club. His goal for Seattle, which is richly illustrated with historic real-photo postcards, is to give readers a deeper appreciation for Seattle's "dynamic and colorful story."

The postcards included in Seattle illustrate some of the interesting historical facets of Washington State's largest city; from the early sky-rise buildings to the mammoth old-growth trees, postcard and history enthusiasts will find enthralling images and information on each page, as the postcard images are each accompanied by detailed descriptions, putting the pictures in context with history. Who isn't in awe at the sight of a tree stump so large it was made into a cabin and lived in?

Seattle is a brief trip into the Pacific Northwest as it once was, from the majesty of its old-growth forests to the energy and excitement of a successful boomtown and beyond.

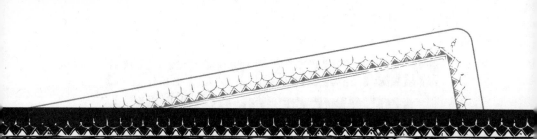

CHAPTER 5

ADS AND ARTIFACTS

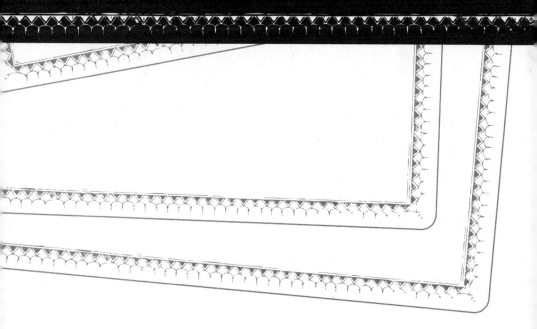

CANDY-THEMED POSTCARDS ARE SWEET TO COLLECT

How many of your happiest childhood memories involve guilt-free indulgence in candy? Chocolate bars, homemade fudge, cotton candy at the county fair, jellybeans and all-day suckers are the comfort food of the young, and it's easy to be nostalgic about enjoying sweet treats without any concern for the consequences.

Fortunately, collectors can enjoy the pursuit of candy without actually eating any. Postcards show that the attitude toward sweets was very different in the early 1900s, many people believing that they were actually good for children (and that it was healthy for children to be plump).

If there's a gene for a raging sweet tooth, my family certainly had it. In fact, my very existence can be traced to my grandfather's urge for a stick of candy. If he hadn't gone into town to buy some, he might not have met the friends who later hooked him up with my grandmother. The rest is history, but candy was always a reward in my childhood. The

The 'Cracker Jack Bears' No. 12.

Were a great success
upon the field
And with effect the
bat can wield,
But playing ball grows
rather slack
When we can eat good
"Cracker Jack"

Lopez — 922 Canal St., New Orleans, La.
A Landmark-where the first Chocolate Bons-Bons
were made in the United States.

scarcity of sugar during World War II made it even more highly prized.

If nostalgia alone isn't enough motivation to seek out postcards about candy, the postcards themselves are. Candy represents pleasure, and the advertising often reflects this.

Nor are the old "goodies" particularly scarce. The best source of information is *American Advertising Postcards, Sets and Series, 1890 to 1920* by Frederic and Mary Megson. This choice reference book devotes more than seven pages to "confectionery," including candy stores and ice cream parlors.

Some of the names in the Megsons' book are still familiar today: Hershey Chocolates, Fralinger's Taffy, Ghirardelli's Chocolates, Huyler's Chocolates, and Cracker Jack. Others are long forgotten: Greenfield's Chocolate Sponge, Hildreth's Velvet Candy, and Mirror Candies, as examples.

Hershey was by far the largest publisher of postcards as advertising, although quite a few only picture the buildings and grounds around their Pennsylvania factory. Many of these are narrow black and white postcards. They're not directly related to their chocolate, nor are they as entertaining as those of some other advertisers. Hershey continued to make postcards in the modern era for their many visitors, including continental size (4 inches by 6 inches) of candy production and candy bars.

Some of the highlights of a candy collection would be: the Cracker Jack Bears (set of 16), Fralinger's Taffy's series of nursery rhymes, and Huyler's Candies' Indian chiefs, girl graduates and girl golfers, to name just a few.

Have another! my Ma says;

"are good for Children"

THE BEAUTIFUL LOUIS XIV CANDY SHOP, Bowes-Allegretti Co., 163 State St., Cor. Monroe, CHICAGO

My favorites are the interiors of candy shops and confectioneries, which also had soda fountains. Almost everything pictured in the early 20th century shops is collectible today.

That includes marble topped counters, caned, bent wood and metal chairs, glass-fronted bins, elaborate soda dispensers, and beautiful ceramic and glass jars. Even empty candy boxes from this era are worth a collector's attention.

Seemingly unrelated scenes were also distributed to call attention to candy products. If there's advertising on the back, the card is a keeper.

It's still possible to put together an impressive album of candy cards, some more enjoyable than a sweet treat and definitely longer lasting.

POSTCARDS DOCUMENT OIL'S WINS, LOSSES

Do you remember when oil was called "black gold" or "Texas tea" in the "Beverly Hillbillies'" theme song? Striking oil was the ultimate source of wealth, more desirable than gold or diamonds. It flowed out of the ground, and no one gave much thought to running out of it.

My home state of Michigan was at least a minor player in the search for underground wealth. One of my father's friends took him to see a rig drilling for oil near Allegan in the late 1940s, and for some forgotten reason, they took me along. His friend, a restaurant owner, wanted to get in on a possible boom. I have no idea why a man who knew very little about the oil business wanted advice from my father, who knew nothing about it, but that's the nature of speculation. For my part, I was disappointed by the metal arm pumping away in a field — no derrick, no great gush of oil shooting into the air.

Of more than 50,000 wells drilled in Michigan, 21,000 were dry holes.

One of the early ones, a Saginaw well drilled in 1925, first produced 23 barrels a day but dwindled to six the second year. This doesn't mean that the state wasn't a viable producer, but it could help explain why my father's friend never struck it rich.

It's not too difficult to find postcards that record this country's oil production. After the discovery of oil in Pennsylvania in 1859, the United States became the world's No. 1 producer and is still the third largest. From Appalachia to Alaska, wealth flowed out of the ground, and it was a cause for celebration.

Oil well postcards have special value, not because they're particularly rare or unusual, but because they reflect the attitude of the American public at the time they were made. Oil production brought wealth to individuals and states and improved the lives of ordinary people. Coal furnaces became obsolete; homeowners no longer had to shovel the dirty black stuff into their furnaces. Oil and natural gas were cleaner, easier and more efficient.

An abundance of petroleum fueled the automobile industry and made horse-drawn vehicles as obsolete as whale oil lamps. This meant cleaner streets, and buildings weren't coated with grime from burning coal. In the 20th century viewpoint, what was not to like about oil?

Postcards from the first half of the last century reflect this acceptance and celebration of petroleum. There were plenty of things to worry about in that century: war, disease, poverty and social ills, but the environmental concerns of today weren't among them. If there's a future for postcards as collectibles — and I firmly believe there is — it lies in their "hidden" value.

As long as people care about history, these small pieces of paper give unique insights into what mattered in the past. Armies of photographers recorded everything that was important to earlier generations, and even the subjects of art add to the total picture of yesteryear.

If you've seen one postcard showing gushing oil, the next one you see won't seem that unique. What matters is what you can't see: How people felt about a new and growing industry in the 20th century.

RECYCLED POSTCARDS: ART OR CRIME?

A friend recently saw several baskets made of postcards at an auction and wondered if postcard collectors were interested in this type of novelty. The answer brings up a major divide between artists who think their art takes precedence and collectors who cherish the ephemera of the past.

Blame Georges Braque and Pablo Picasso.

Early in the 20th century, they took newspaper, wallpaper and other bits of paper and turned them into an exciting new art medium.

Today, collage, from the French word for glue, is an extremely popular art form done by both professionals and amateurs. From then until now, collage artists have seen postcards as raw material for their creations.

In the same period when artists were turning to this new way of creating art, postcards were flooding the nation. Our ancestors were thrifty, tending to keep anything and everything that might be useful some day. Fortunately for us, millions of postcards were saved from destruction

by this reluctance to throw things away. But not all savers were collectors or hoarders. It was only natural that people who loved to do crafts would look around for materials and find postcards.

In fact, some postcards were designed to have things done to them. There were paper doll cards to cut, cute scenes to color and secret

pictures that could only be activated with heat. If these types are scarce today, it's because many were ruined by people having fun with them.

These destructive activities were aimed at children, but adults could also have fun playing with postcards. Leather cards could be assembled into pillows, and pretty Christmas cards were naturals to use as tree

'NIC' ER. R..RESH MILK.'

ornaments. Creative types might turn postcards into baskets, purses or découpage objects, like boxes.

Here's where it gets sticky. Dedicated collectors will feel like weeping if they see wonderful old postcards turned into a lampshade, but collectors of folk art may marvel at the cleverness of the craftsperson who made it.

Is there a middle ground? For one thing, the great majority of people who tucked away postcards from the early 1900s had no idea that they'd ever be valuable. I have to admit that my collection was greatly enriched by both my father's friends and mine who were glad to get rid of old postcards that had been lying around for years. They had no idea that they were giving me valuables, nor did I, since most of the cards in my early collection had been purchased for a penny or so.

It's no wonder, then, that artistic people thought of ways to incorporate family hoards of postcards into their arts and crafts.

But what about today? Thousands of examples of collage art can be found online. This is also true for assemblage art, which is the 3-D version of collage. And yes, postcards are still being sacrificed in the cause of art. I have a foot in both camps. Obviously, I love postcards, but I also do collages and embellish postcards that have nothing to recommend themselves to collectors. It distresses me when I see a really "good" postcard ruined in the cause of art, but billions of postcards have been made in the last hundred years. There is no way that collectors want all of them.

Here are a few simple rules I follow in "embellishing" postcards.

First, they have to be cheap; 25 cents is about my max.

Second, they have to be unpopular with collectors. Black and white art reproductions and unidentified scenes top the list. I look for cards that are so drab that even a fanatical collector would refuse to buy them.

Third, what I add has to improve them. Since I make them for my own enjoyment, this is completely subjective.

I'm not alone as a collector who also enhances otherwise undesirable postcards. A good friend and collector, Louise Northam, now in her nineties, got me started. A creation by Joan Gentry showed me how easy it is to make button-face cards. (It's also easy to affix buttons to old cards and pass them off as originals, but this is never my friends' intent or mine.) It's an unwritten rule to either start from scratch or use cards that no one wants.

If artists are careless about incorporating valuable postcards into their art, they may feel the results justify it. There certainly is a lively market for folk art, and a basket made of postcards might thrill a collector of primitive crafts.

Postcard collectors may feel regret at the sacrifice, but there are more than enough wonderful cards to satisfy every collector.

Restoration of Armored Dinosaur, U.S. National Museum, Smithsonian Institution

COLLECTORS SEARCH FOR PREHISTORIC GIANTS

My brother found a mammoth tooth in a gravel pit when he was a college student working summers on road construction. It was chalky white and beautiful, and I coveted it mightily. I still haven't forgiven his ex-wife for giving it to a neighbor.

Those who follow auction news know that finding prehistoric fossils is like striking gold. Museums and private collectors are willing and eager to pay huge amounts, especially for complete dinosaur skeletons. Alas, it's unlikely that anyone reading this will ever own so much as a toe bone, but dinosaur watching has become a popular activity, especially since "Jurassic Park," and the many TV documentaries. Fortunately for collectors, it is possible to tap into the history of prehistoric creatures through postcards. Museums and other institutions that own complete or nearly complete fossilized skeletons frequently issue postcards to attract visitors and enhance their reputations.

There's potential for finding fossils wherever conditions were right

for preserving them, but the La Brea tar pits, South Dakota badlands and sites in Western states like Utah, Wyoming and Montana have been particularly rich in finds. And perhaps best of all, science has advanced to the point where new knowledge keeps adding to the picture of prehistoric life. Who would have thought of feathered dinosaurs, the probable ancestors of birds? Who knew they hunted in packs? And why wouldn't skeletal remains inspire

Dinosaur Skeleton, 70 feet long, U.S. National Museum, Smithsonian Institution

SINCLAIR DINOSAUR EXHIBIT AT THE CENTURY OF PROGRESS

legends of fierce dragons? There's not much for dinosaur postcard collectors before the 1930s when the Sinclair Oil Company used the brontosaurus as their logo. They created a full-size dinosaur for the Chicago World's Fair in 1933, and several different postcards show this model of a 70-foot long creature, certainly a favorite of visitors who liked to be photographed standing near the giant.

Dinosaur Park near Rapid City, S.D., made a tourist attraction by creating five full-size concrete reproductions of the prehistoric animals that inhabited the region of the Black Hills millions of years ago. Besides a huge brontosaurus, the park features a Tyrannosaurus Rex,

16 feet high and 35 feet long. Scientists now speculate that the fierce monster may actually have been a scavenger and that his small arms weren't much use in a fight. Of course, with teeth like his, who needs claws?

Museums are, of course, the best source for postcards. My favorites are the photographs sold mostly in the 1940s. They're not colorful like later chromes, but every bone stands out, as well as the framework that holds up the massive skeleton. Major museums can't be blamed for the pride they take in fully fossilized dinosaurs, but one of the most dramatic is a Barosaurus on display at the American Museum of Natural History in New York City. (One of their early dinosaur hunters was Roy Chapman Andrews, the inspiration for Indiana Jones.) A plant-eater, it's posed with an incredibly long neck soaring up to a high ceiling. The people viewing it look tiny in comparison.

Somewhere along the line, museum curators decided that prehistoric beasts could be best depicted by giving them skin, fur, eyes, or whatever was needed to make their models seem more real. Once example is shown on a black and white card, possibly from the '30s or '40s, of an "ice-age elephant" that once roamed Minnesota. It was on display in the St. Paul museum. The Smithsonian went a step further when it exhibited an "armored dinosaur" complete with simulated skin, a technique used by other museums too. Among the more common postcards are artist-drawn depictions of dinosaurs. These are mostly chrome cards and include some large enough to frame. As learning tools for children, they're great, but adult enthusiasts may also enjoy them.

Digging up, preserving and moving fragile bones is an art that requires extreme care and patience. The paleontologists who do this are seldom pictured on postcards, but when they are, the cards are real winners. Several scenes from Dinosaur National Monument in Utah feature work in progress.

Although I don't usually collect continental (4×6) postcards, one of my favorite dinosaur-related cards is a modern-size picture of Mary Anning (1799-1847) issued by the British Natural History Museum. At the age of eleven, she found the first complete ichthyosaur in Dorset.

For years she made her living selling fossils she found. She was untrained and unschooled, but she was definitely a pioneer in the field. Those who really want to own a fossil may be able to find the outline of a plant or a small creature imbedded in rock, but the best bet to find the big guys is to hunt them on postcards.

SKULL DRUDGERY PRESERVED FOR POSTERITY ON POSTCARDS

Do you think your job is tough?

Try watching "The Worst Jobs in History," a BBC series with host Tony Robinson actually doing the most unpleasant jobs from six historical periods. If the show doesn't cycle your way in the near future, try the Internet to read about "professions" like mudlarking (sorting through debris at low tide), stone breaking or cesspool cleaning.

The Victorian period, 1832 to 1901, was the last era covered by the series, but the postcards of the early 1900s show that horrible jobs were still plentiful. As a long-time collector of occupation cards, I had no trouble whatsoever putting together a large group showing jobs no one should have to do.

Personal fears make any list of worst jobs subjective. Fear of heights,

Diaconie Weeshuis, Amsterdam. Linnenkamer.

Miners entering Cage, preparatory to being lowered down into Mine, Ironwood Mich.—18

confined spaces, reptiles, insects, or germs might make one job seem the worst of all, but some jobs were so awful that only the poor or desperate would be trapped into doing them. At the top of any list are jobs delegated to children.

Using young people as chimney sweeps or forcing them into the mines were horrendous practices. The latter appeared on postcards in the movement to ban child labor, but most "worst job" cards were made to show how people worldwide eked out a living. No doubt the travelers who bought them felt better about their own lifestyles when compared to the ways some people had to earn a living.

Mining is a dangerous, unpleasant job frequently pictured on old postcards. A hundred years later it's still a hard way to make a living, and mine disasters are always a possibility. There are large numbers of early mining scenes available on postcards, but watch out for generic ones, photographs credited to several different mines. They're worth only a fraction of what an identified mining scene should bring.

Growing and processing food has always been a laborious task. It's hard to picture heat, dirt, wind, drought, sweat and pain on a postcard, but agricultural scenes of homesteaders and small farms sometimes bring alive the hardships.

Some food companies proudly distributed scenes of hygienic assembly lines but the slaughter of animals was also a postcard subject. In surfing Google's 30.6 million references to worst jobs, I found that poultry processing is one of the worst modern jobs; it's nasty, smelly and unpleasant.

People who scavenge for a living (no, not antiques dealers!) are particularly pathetic but less apt to be pictured on a postcard. Only investigative reporters will follow children who live off garbage dumps.

Compulsory work is also hard to find on postcards, especially that of prisoners in chain gangs or doing other hard labor. On the other hand, people in military service, whether volunteers or draftees, were often photographed, although the emphasis was on scenes that reflected well on the government. Some scenes of real-life military life certainly belong on the "worst job" list.

Drudgery was so much a part of a housewife's life a hundred years ago that it took the suffrage movement to bring it to attention. Women's worst jobs on postcards are harder to find than men's, but some are equally unpleasant. Laundry workers, for example, were absolutely necessary in the days before washing machines. Imagine a hot, steamy hell that stinks of chemicals used in soaps and populate it with women working long, hard days.

A favorite postcard scene from some countries also shows washing clothes in rivers or streams, beating them on rocks to get them clean.

Then there was ironing….

Wherever there's glitz and glamour in history, there's a whole army of people slaving away at hard, dirty, dangerous, underpaid job. Look hard and you'll find a lot of them on postcards.

THIS MIGHT SOUND CORNY, BUT IT'S TRUE

One of the incredible things about collecting postcards is that they can mirror a lifetime of varied interests. When I began collecting at age 10, I thought that getting one card from all 48 (yes, 48) states was the pinnacle of success. Then a few foreign cards trickled into my collection from exotic places like Iraq and the Gold Coast, and postcards helped open a worldwide view.

In later years, I had a short-lived mania for all things miniature and began making little room boxes. Naturally, I was wild to find dollhouse and diorama postcards to give "inspiration."

Postcards also helped fill gaps in my education. Somehow I'd never gotten around to taking a course in art appreciation. A large collection of fine art on postcards and a few books filled that void, and I still enjoy

CORN DANCE
ISLETA, NEW MEXICO

PURPLE CROSS
BANTAM CORN

Corn Woman

Stengels and other choice reproductions.

When I went back to another childhood hobby, stamp collecting, I started looking at my postcards for examples of postal history. Today most of the cards I'm adding to my collection have small-town cancellations, preferably with a view of the same town on the front.

There isn't enough space in a single section to list all the topics I've pursued over the years, but undoubtedly the quirkiest is corn.

Until our family moved to Iowa in 1980, corn was something we ate on the cob in the summer. It was culture shock to drive halfway across that state in late August when it seemed to be an ocean of green stalks.

Shortly after we settled in, a little boy was lost in a cornfield for several days in northern Iowa, thankfully found alive. It impressed me so much that I used the incident in the first romance novel I wrote for Dell.

There was much to learn about corn, beginning with the incredible process that filled huge wagons with billions of dried kernels every fall. The price to harvest corn? Even at the time, a farmer might invest a quarter million in an air-conditioned combine.

One son spent six weeks or so in the summer detasseling, a process necessary to produce hybrid seed corn. The other rented a house where the sound of drying corn in a nearby silo went on 24 hours a day during the season.

No wonder then that I began to collect postcards that helped tell the fantastic story of this agricultural gold. The most popular corn cards show the Corn Palace in Mitchell, S.D. Built in 1892 and rebuilt several times, it was embellished with Moorish domes and minarets in 1937. Every year (except 2006 when there was a severe drought) a new design is created over the exterior of the building using corn as the main medium. Early postcards of this constantly changing monument are widely sought. Besides being a huge tourist attraction, the palace is a community center and the site for basketball, rodeo and other events.

There are a surprising number of corn-related postcards. A partial check list includes corn fields; the Corn Exchange bank in Chicago; corn on greetings; advertising including those for corn seed; the corn fence in New Orleans; Native American corn; popcorn wagons; corn planting; harvesting and processing; breakfast cereals made of corn; Cornhusker postcards (Nebraska); old-fashioned corn husking scenes; and comics and exaggerations. There's no limit to the potential of corn as a postcard topic. From the early 1900s to the present, corn shows up with some regularity.

Whether you specialize in early cards, linens or modern, the chances are some choice corn cards are waiting to be found. It remains to be seen whether corn as fuel will ever be portrayed on postcards, but it is certain that corn is increasingly important in a world running short of petroleum products and food.

CHARMING CHILDREN PROMOTED SWIFT'S BUTTERINE

What could be more nourishing for rosy-cheeked children than a liberal helping of sweet creamery butter? Swift, the giant Chicago meat packer used postcards of adorable children in national costumes to promote their alternative: butterine.

What exactly was butterine? In the days before product labeling it was sold as a substitute for real butter, but the contents were a bit obscure. It was made of animal fat with the addition of other ingredients, possibly some milk. It was intended for cooking or as a spread for those who couldn't afford or were too frugal to buy the genuine article.

The savings don't seem impressive today, but in 1902 a penny still had some buying power. A pound of real butter sold from 20 to 25 cents. Butterine was available for 15 to 18 cents a pound, but conscientious mothers had to be convinced that it was wholesome and good for their children. What better way than to associate it with the delightful little girls and their dolls on this set of advertising postcards?

The four known cards show Spanish, Japanese, Dutch and American Indian children and their dolls with small scenes at the top. It's very appropriate that different nationalities were shown. Swift reaped great profits by shipping butterine abroad, but not always with stellar results.

Production of butterine began in 1881, but it soon became a source

INDIAN

Copyright 1908 Swift & Company   Swift's Premium Butterine

of controversy. In Dublin, Ireland an "inspector of nuisances" caught at least three sellers passing butterine off as real butter. One grocer was cautioned, but two others were fined five pounds and ten pounds.

The cases revolved around whether the "butterine" sign was acciden-

JAPANESE

Swift's Premium Butterine

tally or deliberately obscured. A similar case in Britain also resulted in a 5-pound, 5-shilling fine.

The high point for butterine came when it was given an award for good taste, appearance and color at the Chicago World's Fair in 1893. It apparently ceased production under that name when a fire in the Chicago stockyards destroyed the plant manufacturing lard and butterine in 1909.

This was far from the end of the butter substitute controversy. Swift became a major producer of oleomargarine, or margarine, as it's now known. Its sale was bitterly contested by the butter lobby, a movement that began in New York and New Jersey. One early law in New Hampshire required an unappetizing pink color be added, but the Supreme Court struck it down. Still, by 1900, 80% of Americans couldn't buy margarine with yellow food coloring added. Some manufacturers supplied food coloring to be added by the consumer.

The lower price of margarine kept it on grocery shelves, and butter shortages during World War I made it especially popular. Butter regained lost ground during the Great Depression, but margarine soared in sales during World War II. During this time my mother tried mixing yellow food coloring into white margarine in a big bowl, a rather messy and time-consuming process. However the substitute spread didn't please my father and soon disappeared from our table.

Eventually the laws against colored margarine were relaxed. In 1967, Wisconsin was the last state to capitulate.

Swift also issued a set of six butterine advertising postcards featuring children with airships. They also promoted their oleomargarine with another three sets designed with child-appeal. Postcards can also be found advertising their meat projects, but the butterine cards are certainly more appealing than the meat packing scenes, supposedly showing how sanitary and efficient their processing was.

Regardless of whether butterine had any appeal as a butter substitute, the advertising postcards have lasting charm and collectibility.

THE OTHER BASEBALL CARDS

For those who love baseball collectibles but find the traditional "bubblegum" cards too pricey or too commercial, there's a pleasant alternative: BASEBALL POSTCARDS.

It isn't possible to find a postcard of every major league player who ever picked up a bat, but there are a surprising number of really nice cards for collectors who like searching for sports gems.

Major league stadiums are a good place to begin. In the 1930s and '40s most, if not all, stadiums appeared on linen postcards, the best of which show an interior view with spectators and a game in progress.

Players are more likely to be found on later cards, especially standard-size chromes of the '50s and '60s. The Baseball Hall of Fame is another good source for player postcards.

There's a lot more to baseball than the highly organized professional teams of today. The game evolved gradually from folk games that date back as early as the 14th century in Europe. In the United States, Abner Doubleday has largely been discredited as the inventor of the game. Rather, baseball as it's played in modern times, gradually grew into a national mania with American roots in the 19th century.

The first rules were published for the New York Knickerbockers in 1845, and later in the century Brooklyn had the first fenced fields that allowed backers to charge admission to games. In the early years, the players were amateurs playing for fun, but in 1869 the Cincinnati Red Stockings became the first professional team, recruiting players and traveling to find competition.

The Civil War did much to spread the game as bored soldiers and prisoners filled idle hours by playing a version of baseball. Whatever the history of the organized sport, it caught on in the late 19th and early 20th centuries. Baseball fields became a traditional in towns and villages across the country.

Perhaps the best of all baseball postcards are those that document hometown teams playing for fun. If a sandlot player made it to the big leagues, he brought fame and glory to the people back home. But for every star, there were thousands and thousands of men and boys (and later girls playing mostly softball) whose lives were enriched by the game.

The sport spread to schools, military groups, semi-pro teams and even prisons. Basically it became an all-American recreation, and groups that were proud of their teams would record them on postcards. Like the team photos taken today, real photos of teams were mainly distributed to players and their families, making many of these scarce and choice.

Some particularly entertaining baseball cards show House of David teams. They barnstormed the country from the 1920s to 1955 playing both amateur and semi-pro competitors. Benjamin Purnell founded the religious cult in 1903, and weekend baseball began in 1913. The teams were one of many commercial efforts, and by the early 1920s better players were being hired. They didn't have to join the cult, but they were required to play with long hair.

The House of David was split after scandals in the late 1920s but still fielded up to three teams. They owned a financial empire that included a popular amusement park where postcards could be purchased. (My mother-in-law was a close friend of a member who left the cult – the source of my interest.)

For those who don't take baseball seriously, there are many baseball comics including some featuring children. Perhaps best of all, there's always the chance of finding a rare or unusual image. Baseball has been part of the American scene for a long time, and the "other" baseball cards are well worth the attention of collectors.

POSTCARDS HELP PRESERVE AN OLD WORLD FOLK ART: FAN-CARVING

From the editors of Antique Trader

Postcards are being used to help preserve an almost lost folk art, that of fan-carving. The most culturally significant fan-carved item is the fan bird.

The fan bird represents the dove of peace. It is a three-dimensional design made from one piece of wood. Fan-carving is an Old World folk art that came to America with Scandinavian immigrants.

To the Europeans, the fan bird is known by many names: Holy Spirit, bird of inspiration, dove of peace, Christmas bird, Easter bird, chip dove, cuckoo, splint bird, etc. Traditionally, the fan bird is hung in the home by a string so it may move freely with air currents. It seems to some alive and symbolizes protection, health, and happiness for the family.

A fan-carved dove was found in many Scandinavian churches in the 17th century. It hung in the pulpit directly over the minister's head, hence the name pulpit bird.

By the 1900s, the fan bird seemed to be everywhere throughout Scandinavia and Europe. In fact, two distinguished ethnographers proclaimed it a cultural phenomenon.

However, as time passed, fewer local artisans made fan birds. In time, the pulpit bird was even replaced by a solid wooden dove. There are few fan birds being made in Europe and Scandinavia today. In some countries they can only be found in museums or archival documents.

This Old World folk art along with its rich and meaningful symbolism almost became lost, but it is now enjoying a renaissance due to the fan-carvers of today.

Sally and David Nye are world renowned for their tireless efforts in

researching and preserving the Old World folk art of fan-carving.

Their research has taken them across Europe and Scandinavia. The Nyes soon found themselves in the unique position of teaching the Europeans their heritage about the fan bird, along with its legends and customs.

Sally and David have recorded this symbolism and history in their books: Fan-Carving and More Fan-Carving.

It is their hope that the postcards shown here will bring attention to fan-carving and help preserve it.

THE LEGEND OF THE FAN BIRD

During the Medieval Era, families lived in one-room log houses that were covered with clay inside and out. There was just one window, covered with a dried animal stomach, during the winter and a small smoky stone fireplace.

One family in northern Russia lived in such a house with a young boy who was very ill. He lay on his bed where he was covered with furs. People came from neighboring villages to try to help him regain his health, but all efforts were in vain.

It was the end of winter, and his father was sitting by the fireplace making baskets. Tired of lying in a stuffy house, the ill boy asked, "Dad, is summer coming soon?"

His father replied, "Soon, son, very soon. Just a little more and summer will be here."

Then his father got an idea. He thought, "I will make a bird from this piece of wood. I will make it to look like a real bird with two wings and a tail. Maybe my son will think summer has come and the birds have returned. That would make him very happy."

The father said, "I will make summer for you."

He made a bird and hung it from the ceiling near the fireplace where his son could see it. The draft of the hot air streams from the fire caused the bird to spin. Its wings began to move and suddenly it became alive.

The son was filled with joy and his health improved. The people from the neighboring villages returned to ask how the boy was healed. When they heard the story about the bird, they asked the father to make a bird for their home to safeguard and protect their family.

Thus, the bird assumed magical powers and became known as the "Holy Ghost," safekeeper of children and symbol of family happiness.

POSTCARDS WAGE PROPAGANDA WAR ON PROHIBITION

Charles Bush

Water, water, every where, And all the boards did shrink. Water, water, every where, Nor any drop to drink.

— *"The Rime of the Ancient Mariner," Samuel Taylor Coleridge, 1834*

Did you know that it was the Puritans that initiated America's love affair with alcohol? It's true! When the Mayflower docked at Plymouth Rock, her hold was filled with kegs of beer, not water – and for good reason. The Puritans were coming to the New World from Europe. In Europe at that time, sanitary engineering was almost non-existent. As a result, European public water supplies were often contaminated with the bacteria that caused epidemics of cholera and typhoid fever. Beer, wine and distilled spirits all contained enough alcohol to kill these bacteria and were therefore much safer to drink than water. Over-indulgence of alcohol to the point of public drunkenness, however, was still considered a sin against God.

As America grew and prospered, the majority of its population remained engaged in hard physical labor that worked up quite a thirst. Since old habits were hard to break, thirst was quenched with beer, hard cider and, of course, Demon Rum. As time passed, public drunkenness became more prevalent. Soon alcohol consumption became associated not only with public disorder but also with insanity, poverty and various types of criminal behavior. More importantly, the use of alcohol was thought to be the cause of the disintegration of social values and the family unit.

It was in this atmosphere that the Temperance Movement was born.

Women and religious leaders became involved in a campaign for moderation in the consumption of intoxicating beverages. Initially, propaganda and moral suasion were used to address the problem.

Following the Civil War, abolitionists, who had fought to abolish slavery, went looking for new social causes to support. Well-organized and politically savvy, they joined the ranks of the Temperance Movement preaching abstinence and prohibition rather than moderation.

At this same time, America was experiencing a great influx of immigrants from Europe, including hundreds of thousands of Germans who brought with them their own love for beer.

By 1874, the same year in which the white ribbons of the National Women's Christian Temperance Union first appeared, there were more than 4,000 breweries in the United States. Most of these breweries were local operations with a relatively small customer base. However, with improvements in brewing technology and the advent of refrigerated railcars, some breweries, like the Pabst Brewing Co. of Milwaukee, Wis., became industry giants. The Anheuser-Busch Association of St. Louis, Mo., opened its doors to the public for guided tours and even sponsored floats in Pasadena's Tournament of Roses Parade.

As the popularity of beer grew, particularity in the cities where many of the European immigrants had congregated for employment, many of the larger breweries began to open saloons.

Despite fierce competition, enormous profits could be made by selling beer and liquor by the glass rather than by the bottle. Saloons proliferated. By the early 1890s, there was one saloon for every 200 persons living in the United States. The saloon was a man's world, and the only women allowed were strictly for the purpose of entertainment.

Such unrestrained growth by the "purveyors of alcohol," combined with the "immoral activities" such as gambling and prostitution that were attributed to all saloons, certainly caught the attention of the Temperance Movement. In 1893, the Anti-Saloon League of America (ASLA) was founded by Howard Hyde Russell. Russell was a lawyer who had experienced a religious conversion and had become a minister in the Congregational Church. As a Temperance zealot, Russell used his organizational skills and his political influence to promote the Prohibitionist agenda.

While Russell chose to sway public opinion by flooding the market with propaganda in the form of books, journals, magazines articles and postcards, another Temperance reformer was taking a somewhat more direct approach.

From 1900 to 1910, Carrie Nation and her hatchet cut a swath of destruction through Kansas saloons. Arrested more than 30 times, Nation typically paid her fines with proceeds from the sale of souvenir hatchets.

With the advent of World War I, anti-German sentiment within the United States began to build. It reached a peak in 1917 with America's entry into the War. As beer sales fell, Prohibitionists turned up the heat on politicians to outlaw the manufacture of all alcoholic beverages. On January 16, 1919, Nebraska became the 36th state to ratify the 18th Amendment to the Constitution, and exactly one year later, the Noble Experiment of Prohibition began.

The Volstead Act was passed by Congress to enforce the terms of Prohibition. Created by Prohibitionists, the new law was much more severe than the general public had been led to believe it would be. Worst of all, it forbid the manufacturing of beer with more than 0.5 percent alcohol content (beers produced prior to the enactment of Prohibition typically contained from 3 to 6 percent alcohol). As a result, the majority of the breweries in America shut down operations to the utter delight of the Prohibitionists. However, their celebration would be short-lived.

The large breweries like Busch, Pabst and Schmidt's all modified their brewing processes to produce the permitted low alcohol content beer commonly known as "near beer."

Other breweries diversified. In addition to producing three brands of near beer, the country's oldest brewery, the Yuengling Brewing Co. of Pottsville, Pa., opened a dairy and sold ice cream. The Schlitz Brewing Co. changed its name to the Schlitz Beverage Company and tried its hand at selling chocolate bars – a disastrous venture that ended up costing the company more than $15 million.

Determined not to be denied their beer, many Americans turned to making beer at home, an activity that remained perfectly legal. Some merely added other forms of alcohol to near beer. That proved dangerous, as certain types of alcohol (like wood alcohol) caused blindness and even death. Others tried their hand at actually brewing beer from scratch at home. This task was made easier when several of the major breweries that continued to operate began selling malt extract (sometimes called "wort") to the public.

The malt extract was sold ostensibly for the purpose of baking muffins. In 1923 alone, statistics showed that Americans made more than 80 million hops-flavored malt muffins.

The home brewing craze was memorialized by a member of the New York Rotary Club who wrote: "Mother's in the kitchen washing out the jugs; Sister's in the pantry bottling the suds; Father's in the cellar mixing up the hops; Johnny's on the front porch watching for the cops."

As other countries chuckled at America's Noble Experiment, the Temperance Movement began to lose both popularity and support. Americans wanted their beer back.

When the stock market crashed in 1929 and Depression enveloped the country, the population lost all patience with temperance and began to demand an end to Prohibition. In March 1933, President Franklin Roosevelt signed the Cullen-Harrison Act allowing the manufacture and sale of beer containing 3.2 percent alcohol.

Finally, on Dec. 5, 1933, the 21st Amendment to the Constitution, which repealed the 18th Amendment, was ratified and Prohibition came to an end. After 13 long years, beer was back and Americans sang "Happy Days Are Here Again."

THE STYLIZED REALISM OF CATHARINA KLEIN

Joseph Truskot

Gooseberries!

That's what they were, hanging from a thorny branch like paper lanterns. I found the postcard in a thrift store in Elyria, Ohio, in 1971 and bought it because a college friend grew a variety of this once common fruit called Pixwell. But it was the card's design that intrigued me most. The fruit was painted realistically, and yet with style. I loved it.

Thirty-five years passed.

My postcard collecting was in fits and starts with multi-year intervals of quiet. I bought a house with a yard, became interested in roses, and once again dragged down my collection to see what flower cards I owned. The Internet became a source of new cards at reasonable prices. By searching for roses, I found and bought several bearing the "C. Klein" signature. They were, by far, the most breathtaking roses I'd ever seen painted and they were on postcards.

Simple searches for "C. Klein" produced more and more examples of her astonishing output: flowers, birds, butterflies, fruit, and still life scenes – all displaying her characteristic inventiveness. I found conflicting information about her though, so I wrote to libraries in Germany for some facts on this phenomenal person whose work seemed to be everywhere but whose life is nearly forgotten.

"C. Klein," her trademark signature, stands for Catharina Klein. She is also referred to as Catherine Klein, but that's not a name she ever used herself. Publishers anglicized her name during World War I to avoid any disinclination against buying her work because she was a German national and enormously popular on our side of the trenches.

She is sometimes wrongly referred to as "Christine." Her signature, "C. Klein" usually accompanies her work, especially in those postcards and prints closest to the original paintings, which were in oil or gouache, an opaque watercolor. If her signature is underlined, it's an indication of an earlier work. Klein rode the crest of chromolithography at the end of the 19th and into the 20th century. Millions of copies of her paintings were made. They appeared in book illustrations, on calendars, advertisements, bookmarks, and postcards. They were put on stencils and fired onto teacups. They were converted into patterns and embroidered onto pillowcases.

Catharina Klein was born in 1861 in Eylau, East Prussia, a town now called Bagrationovsk in Kalinigrad, a part of the Russian Federation on Poland's northeast border. (It is actually separated by the Baltic States from Mainland Russia.) Its population couldn't have been more than 3,500 or so when she was a child, thus making her quite well acquainted with rural life and the subject matter she would so beautifully capture on canvas and paper.

Catharina Klein moved to Berlin where she studied at the vocational school. In her earliest days, she exhibited at various shows and her paintings proved popular among the German nobility. Prophetically, one of her paintings was exhibited as part of the Columbia Exhibition in Chicago in 1893 when she was 32. (The Columbia Exhibition is often heralded as the catalyst of the postcard craze.) Klein became one of the most respected and popular still life painters of all time. She captured the essence of her subject matter and made it appealing on a 3 1/2-inch by 5 1/2-inch card.

Occasionally, an early oil painting will come to a German auktion-haus. During the past 10 years, I found documentation on only three original paintings for sale. All listed for less than $1,000. Also on the market, and listed as being hers, were several copies of her works done by students, which are clearly inferior and only have value as curiosities.

A popular teacher, Klein also ran a studio in Berlin and trained young women how to paint. In 1911, she published two short books: one on how to paint fruit, the other flowers. She was a single woman

from the country in a male dominated world and she earned her living through her talent, which was a remarkable feat for that period. She died in Berlin in 1929.

Ever industrious and clearly in demand, Catharina Klein submitted paintings to several publishers. According to Don Barnard's encyclo-pedic work Catharina Klein: A Postcard Catalogue, published in 1998, Klein painted more than 2,250 different still life images and had 75 major publishing companies, and several smaller ones, producing her work. Her best paintings appear on cards printed by Meissner & Buch of Leipzig. She was their star, accounting for 20 percent of their total output creating about 1,000 different works for them. Meissner & Buch used good card stock and expensive ink, which is why many of these 100-year-old pieces of paper are still in excellent condition. Quality cards also came from the large printing firm of G.O.M. (Obpacker Brothers, Munich), a couple of Swiss firms, several other German firms, and Adolphe Tuck of London. (Adolphe and his father Rafael were Germans prospering in England and had no problem securing Klein's work from the Fatherland.)

Once her paintings were delivered and she was paid, the publishers could do what they wished with her work and often resold them to other publishers. This accounts for why the same design was produced by different publishers. Many printers often embellished her work by altering the backgrounds, embossing the image, giving it a linen finish, or printing just an enlarged detail of the original work. The larger her signature is in proportion to the card, the greater the likelihood that the card depicts only a detail of a painting.

Much of Klein's work appeared prior to 1906 when the reverse side of a postcard was intended for the address only. The message appeared on the front. Her artwork was often printed to one side to leave room for a message or, with work intended to be printed on a postcard, Klein displayed phenomenal ingenuity by creating designs with open spaces for a message. After 1906, postcard backs had space available for both a message and an address, thus leaving the beautiful front, unmarred by handwriting. Actually, handwriting on a pre-1906 C. Klein card is considered normal and doesn't affect the price too much.

Chromolithography allowed publishers to manipulate the original art; take figs from one design, for instance, and a crock from another, overprint them on yet another design and come up with a new piece of art to sell. The card was recognizable as work by the artist. In Klein's case, these bizarre concoctions can be spotted because the components are out of proportion to one another. Usually, the light is also wrong. Aware of this practice, Klein frequently placed her signature close to her subject matter (instead of at a bottom corner which could easily be omitted in reproductions). Like all great artists, Klein knew how good she was and a signature appearing on every work contributed to her self-promotion. If a postcard looks like her work but doesn't have a signature, be skeptical. Most have one. Klein's gouache paintings exist now only on postcards, calendars, and advertisements. Where are the originals? The scarcity today of such a vast output may be due to the two world wars. Several warehouses, which may have contained Klein's originals in London, Berlin and Leipzig, were burned to the ground during these conflicts.

Klein also had an avid following among amateur painters, many of whom used her flower and fruit paintings as models for their efforts at painting plates. As late as 1970, The China Decorator magazine was still publishing her advice on what paints to use to achieve various effects, such as the transparency of grapes. Occasionally, a hurricane lamp or dish will turn up with her signature on it. I've found no documentation that she ever used glass or porcelain as her canvas.

Sadly, in the 1950s, an investigation of her gravesite took place. As no relatives were known to have visited her and the art establishment (whoever they were) decided she wasn't significant enough to have her grave preserved, they dug her up and destroyed the remains so that someone else might be buried in her spot.

Even more tragic, several buyers of her postcards today cut them up to make jewelry, scrapbooks, or decoupage wall hangings, thus destroying what could be the only remaining copy of this brilliant artist's work. Admittedly, some Klein designs are ubiquitous but others are quite rare.

Recent auctions of her cards have fetched close to the $250 mark. Most, however, can still be had for under $20. Catharina Klein is a postcard collector's dream, or nightmare, depending on one's success rate at acquiring complete sets of her creations. I know from personal experience, having just 25 of the 26 letters of her flower alphabet escalated my willingness to spend serious money when that missing "Z" finally came on the market!

Klein painted real life subject matter. In doing so, she unintentionally documented examples of fruits and flowers grown during her lifetime, varieties we now consider heirlooms.

Which brings me back to the gooseberries. My original card bore no signature. It was printed in America, postmarked 1919, and was most likely a copy of a copy of a copy of the original. Turns out, it originally came from Meissner & Buch, Series 1287, Fruchtspenden ("A Donation of Fruit"). Its set mates were plums, blackberries, and cherries, arranged similarly. Imagine my thrill when, after all these years, I realized those sentimental gooseberries that I liked years ago came from the hand of a person I now admire so much, the great Catharina Klein.

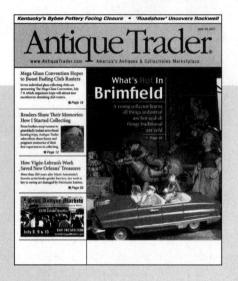